The
Holocaust

Look for these and other books in the Lucent
Overview series:

Abortion
Acid Rain
AIDS
Animal Rights
The Beginning of Writing
Cancer
Dealing with Death
Drugs and Sports
Drug Trafficking
Eating Disorders
Endangered Species
Energy Alternatives
Extraterrestrial Life
Garbage
Gun Control
Hazardous Waste
The Holocaust
Homeless Children
Ocean Pollution
Oil Spills
The Olympic Games
Ozone
Population
Rainforests
Smoking
Special Effects in the Movies
Teen Alcoholism
The UFO Challenge
Vietnam

The Holocaust

by Abraham Resnick

LUCENT
B·O·O·K·S

LUCENT Overview Series

Library of Congress Cataloging-in-Publication Data

Resnick, Abraham, 1924-
    The Holocaust / by Abraham Resnick.
        p.   cm. — (Lucent overview series)
    Includes bibliographical references and index.
    Summary: Discusses the events surrounding the imprisonment and
execution of millions of Jews in Nazi concentration camps during
World War II, and the establishment of a Jewish state in Palestine
following the war.
    ISBN 1-56006-124-3
    1. Holocaust, Jewish (1939-1945)—Juvenile literature.
[1. Holocaust, Jewish (1939-1945)]   I. Title.   II. Series.
D804.3.R48   1991
940.53'18—dc20   91-441

Printed in the U.S.A.

With great admiration and gratitude for those Bulgarians who demonstrated exemplary compassion and courage in helping to save all fifty thousand Bulgarian Jews during the tragic years of the Holocaust era.

Acknowledgments

The author would like to express his appreciation to those who provided assistance and information during the preparation of this book:

International Center for Holocaust Studies
Anti-Defamation League of B'nai B'rith
823 United Nations Plaza
New York, NY 10017

The Nahum Goldman Museum of the Jewish Diaspora
Tel Aviv, Israel

Simon Wiesenthal Center
9760 West Pico Boulevard
Los Angeles, CA 90035

Social, Cultural, and Educational Organization of
Bulgarian Jews
Sofia, Bulgaria

United States Holocaust Memorial Council
2000 L Street NW, Suite 588
Washington, DC 20036-4907

Yad Vashem
Martyrs' and Heroes' Remembrance Authority
Jerusalem, Israel

Contents

Introduction

A HOLOCAUST IS A DISASTER that results in the large-scale destruction of life. Although the term has been used to describe many catastrophes over the centuries, today it has a more specific meaning. The Holocaust refers to the annihilation of millions of Jews and other peoples by Adolf Hitler's Nazi Germany during World War II. Such destruction of a particular race of people or their culture is called *genocide*. The word is formed from the Greek word *genos*, meaning "race" or "nation," and the Latin suffix *cide*, meaning "to kill."

The extermination of the Jews by the Nazis was different than most other examples of genocide in history. The Holocaust was not the result of a power struggle between two opposing groups, a competition for land and resources, a holy crusade, or an attempt to defeat an enemy in order to win a war. Instead, the Jews were put to death simply because they were Jews. The Nazis believed that the Jews were inferior to most other peoples and sought to literally wipe them from the face of the earth.

This was not the first time the Jews had experienced persecution. In fact, through all of their nearly four thousand year history as a people, they had suffered almost constantly from the effects of hatred and bigotry. These attitudes toward

(opposite page) The Holocaust culminated in the systematic execution of over six million European Jews. Here, inmates of the infamous Dachau concentration camp stand for roll call.

Jews are called anti-Semitism. The Biblical Jews were slaves in Egypt and their cities and temples were destroyed by both the Babylonians and Romans. During the crusades of the Middle Ages, Christian soldiers massacred thousands of Jews in an attempt to annihilate all non-Christians. In the centuries that followed, laws in every European country forbade Jews from owning land, so most Jews learned to live in the cities. Other laws kept Jews from living in the same areas as non-Jews, forcing many Jews to live in separate, sealed-off sections of the cities, called ghettos. Because they could not make their living from the land as most other people did, Jews became peddlers, merchants, jewelers, and money lenders.

Clinging to traditional prejudices

By the twentieth century, many people had come to believe that this age-old anti-Semitism was wrong and unjust. Yet there were still some individuals, Adolf Hitler and other Nazi leaders among them, who clung to the traditional prejudices and looked upon the Jews as somehow less than human. When the Nazis came to power in Germany in the 1930s, they began to round up German Jews and send them to concentration camps, where mass numbers of Jews were confined and often forced to perform hard labor. Many of those sent to these camps died there or were later transported to extermination camps, or death camps as they were called.

After the outbreak of World War II, as the Nazis conquered much of Europe, they systematically arrested and murdered Jews from many other countries. The methods of these mass murders included poison gas, hanging, firing squads, and inhumane medical experiments. Most of the bodies were burned in the ovens of huge crematories at death camps like Auschwitz in southern

Poland. In all, the Nazis killed nearly six million Jews between 1933 and 1945.

The Jews were not the only people persecuted and exterminated by Hitler and his regime, however. At least 250,000 Gypsies, a wandering race of people who also suffered from age-old bigotry, were murdered. In addition, another five million non-Jews, thought by the Nazis to be inferior for one reason or another, met their deaths in Hitler's camps. Among these were homosexuals, members of certain religious sects such as Jehovah's Witnesses, and physically and mentally handicapped persons.

The Holocaust has become a symbol of brutality and of one people's inhumanity to another. The catastrophe is still widely discussed, studied, and dramatized in films and on television in hopes that no one will ever forget what happened. Many people fear that, if the disaster is forgotten, such crimes might be repeated. In the words of philosopher Emil Fackenheim, "Civilization must struggle with the memory of the Holocaust because it cannot afford to bury it."

Jews were not the only people exterminated by the Nazis. Gypsies were among the non-Jews who were rounded up and sent to concentration camps.

1

Adolf Hitler and the Rise of Nazi Germany

ADOLF HITLER WAS BORN on April 20, 1889, in the small Austrian town of Braunau-am-Inn. As a child, Hitler was lonely and unhappy and spent much of his time alone. He had a hard time making friends, a trait that continued throughout his life. Despite his father's wish that he become a government worker, the young Hitler aspired to become an artist. Although he was Austrian by birth, some of his relatives were German and Hitler liked to think of himself as German. This was partly because of his fascination with German history, especially the myths of the glorious, blond Aryan Teutonic knights and gods that the German composer Richard Wagner portrayed in his operas. Short with dark hair, Hitler certainly did not look like the ideal Aryan, yet he fancied himself a member of that fanciful, superior race.

Hitler was not a good student. He was argumentative and placed most of the blame for his poor record on his teachers. At the age of sixteen, two years after the death of his father, Hitler dropped out of school, claiming he was unable to

(opposite page) Adolf Hitler is flocked by thousands at a Nazi rally in Bueckburg, 1934.

13

The son of a customs broker, Adolf Hitler was born in 1889 in Braunau-am-Inn, Austria.

continue because of lung trouble. For three years, he roamed about aimlessly, occasionally trying his hand at painting.

When he was nineteen, Hitler set out for Vienna, the capital of Austria, to enroll in the Arts Academy. Because of the poor quality of his work, however, his application was rejected. His evaluation claimed that he was untalented as an artist.

For the next four years, Hitler barely made a living working as a laborer and painting cheap postcards. He was poor and homeless, often living in lower-class rooming houses and eating in charity soup kitchens. He spent much of his time reading German history and philosophy and anti-Jewish literature. Ironically, many of the homeless shelters where he stayed were founded and supported by a Jewish baron. And Hitler received his only warm coat from a Jewish clothes merchant who took pity on him.

Hitler as a young man

In 1912, unhappy in Vienna, Hitler moved to Germany, the country he had long admired. He took up residence in Munich, but his life-style hardly changed. He continued to drift and occasionally work as a carpenter or poster painter. Finding friends in his newly adopted city remained difficult for him and he was alone much of the time. What he enjoyed most was finding small groups of Germans who would listen to his political ideas. He particularly liked to rant about Germany's "enemies," the Jews and the Communists.

At the outbreak of World War I in 1914, Hitler enlisted in an army infantry regiment in Bavaria, a state in southern Germany. Showing great patriotism, he declared his readiness to die for "his" German people. He served in the army for four years as a message carrier, and fought at the front against the British. He was temporarily blinded by poison gas during a battle and was once hospitalized for battle fatigue and shell shock. Eventually, he received the Iron Cross medal for bravery. However, during his military career, Hitler was able to reach only the rank of corporal, a fairly low grade for a soldier. He desperately wanted to become an officer, and when he could not, he became very resentful.

Hitler was equally bitter when Germany was defeated by the Allies in World War I, and he agonized over that loss for many years. After losing the war, the humiliated Germans were forced to sign the Treaty of Versailles in 1919, bringing World War I to a close. The terms of the treaty were harsh. Germany was forced to give some of its richest industrial territories to the victors. It was also made to pay reparations to the Allied countries it had devastated in the war. Germany lost prestige, pride, wealth, power, and the status of being one of Europe's greatest countries. Poverty and hard times swept over Germany.

During World War I, Hitler served as a soldier in the German army.

Hard times in post-World War I Germany

After World War I, Germany, like the rest of Europe, was trying desperately to rebuild and recover from the war. Along with the harsh penalties of the Treaty of Versailles, Germany was also severely affected by the Great Depression. Unemployment and hunger increased. Inflation soared until one billion marks—the German unit of currency—were needed to equal one prewar mark. People had to carry sacks of money to purchase items. A potato sack crammed full of money was needed to buy a pair of shoes. Factories closed and savings were wiped out. In many respects, these terrible economic conditions made Hitler's rise to power possible. In these desperate times,

Hitler at a Nazi party rally at Nuremberg, Germany.

the German people were ready for a leader who would give them a way out. Hitler offered the German people hope. But he intertwined this hope with vicious anti-Semitism.

Hitler placed the blame for Germany's devastated condition partly on the Allied nations who had won the war—England, France, and the United States. But he also blamed others. He firmly believed that the German army had not been fairly defeated in battle, but instead, had been betrayed by the trickery of Communists and Jews, the "evil partners" of the Allies. In Hitler's twisted mind, the rich merchants and international bankers, most of them Jews, had sold Germany out to the enemy. So, he concluded, the Jews were responsible for most of the country's problems. It was at this time that Hitler formed his plans to get revenge someday on the Jews and other enemies of the German people.

When the war ended, Hitler remained in the army. While stationed in Munich, he attended political meetings of the many small groups that had organized to gain control of the government. Hitler's job was to gather information about these groups and relay it to certain army officers who were also planning to seize power. One night in 1919, while spying on six members of the German Workers' party at a dark little restaurant, Hitler suddenly found himself in support of their views. He immediately joined the group and became its spokesman.

The growth of Nazism

By 1921, the Workers' party had changed its name to the Nazi party. The word Nazi was abbreviated from the National Socialist German Workers' party. The group was composed of a small private army of discontented, unemployed veterans and tough, violent hoodlums. At the outset, the members wore brown shirts and carried weapons. Their arm bands sported the swastika, a mystic symbol of ancient origin. This emblem was in the shape of a cross with each arm bent back in a ninety-degree angle and pointing clockwise. Indicating the four directions of the earth, the swastika implied world conquest and also served as a symbol of anti-Semitism.

At Nazi party meetings, Hitler demonstrated his ability to hold his audience spellbound. His vocal cords had been scarred by wartime mustard gas so his voice was harsh and raspy. Hitler possessed a natural charisma before crowds and people could not help but pay attention to what he said. His boisterous speeches, accompanied by wild hand and arm gestures, made people take notice. It was not long before he became the head of the Nazi party.

Often, when he spoke, Hitler provoked extreme reactions. Sometimes, his audiences would become so impassioned that fights would erupt be-

Hitler captivates crowds at a rally in Dortmund, Germany, in 1933. A powerful orator, Hitler offered hope to Germans suffering from the harsh terms of the Treaty of Versailles.

tween his ardent supporters and those who hated his speeches. His views were so outrageous that, at first, many people laughed at him and did not take him seriously. Some were sure that he was mentally unbalanced. Friedrich Reck-Malleczewen, a well-to-do German businessman, described meeting Hitler at the house of a friend in 1920:

> A jellylike, slag-gray face, a moon-face into which two melancholy jet-black eyes had been set like raisins. So sad, so unutterably insignificant, so basically misbegotten. . . . He had come to a house, where he had never been before, wearing gaiters, a floppy, wide-brimmed hat, and carrying a riding whip. . . . Eventually, he managed to launch into a speech. He talked on and on, endlessly. He preached. He went on at us like a division Chaplain in the Army. We did not in the least contradict him, or venture to differ in any way, but he began to bellow at us. The servants thought we were being attacked, and rushed in to defend us. . . . When he had gone, we sat silently confused. . . . There was a feeling of dismay, as when on a train you suddenly find you are sharing a compartment with a psychotic. . . . It was not that an unclean body had been in the room, but something else: the unclean essence of a monstrosity.

Although many, like Reck-Malleczewen, saw Hitler for the sick person that he was, Hitler's tactics increased his visibility. He sent out his armed thugs, called storm troopers, to break up the meetings of Communists and others who opposed him, and convinced great numbers of Germans that he could seize and successfully manipulate power. "Brutality is respected," Hitler later told a German politician. "Brutality and physical strength. . . . The people need wholesome fear. They *want* to fear something. . . . Why babble about brutality and be indignant about tortures? The masses want that. They need something that will give them a thrill of horror." As his followers swelled in number, he became more and more of a threat to those who did not agree with him.

By 1923, the Nazis had ten thousand storm troopers in their ranks. Hitler had become so powerful that he even attempted to overthrow the German government. This attempt failed and the Nazi leader spent eight months in prison. But the uprising demonstrated that Hitler could organize and lead the Nazi storm troopers.

Hitler's pursuit of power

During his 1923 jail term, Hitler wrote *Mein Kampf*, or *My Struggle*, a book recounting much of his life and expressing his personal views. Much of what is known about his early years stems from this emotional autobiography. As historian William L. Shirer commented, "Adolf Hitler had a mystical sense of his personal mission on earth in those days." In *Mein Kampf*, Hitler wrote, "From millions of men . . . *one* man must step forward, who . . . will form granite principles . . . and take up the struggle for their sole correctness, until . . . there will arise a brazen cliff of

A group of German children greet Hitler.

solid unity in faith and will." Hitler believed that these "correct principles" were those of Nazism and that he himself would be the "one" to step forward and lead the world.

Gradually, in the years after he was released from prison, events began to turn in Hitler's favor. Hitler was able to tap a deep well of nationalism in the German people. In highly emotional speeches, Hitler stressed the need for complete loyalty to the fatherland, Germany. He told the people that showing a strong love of country could reestablish Germany as a formidable world power. Hitler called the German people a master Aryan race. According to Hitler, an Aryan was a white person of non-Jewish descent. A pure Aryan would look Nordic or Scandinavian and have a

A page from a children's picture book compares the physical traits of a German (left) and a Jew. Nazism taught that the blond, Nordic features of the Aryan race were superior to all others.

An anti-Semitic newspaper from 1934 accuses the Jews of causing the ills plaguing German society.

long head, a tall body, blond hair, and blue eyes. Since many Germans fit this description, Hitler was able to establish a sense of pride and superiority in the German people. He also promised to put people back to work, to reopen the factories and rebuild Germany's industries.

With six million Germans out of work and millions more unable to buy adequate food, Hitler's promises made him widely popular. In 1932, the Nazis received the highest number of votes in the national election. The German president, the weak and aged Paul von Hindenburg, was forced to appoint Hitler to the position of chancellor. Also swept into power were 230 of Hitler's "brownshirts," his most loyal storm troopers. Having won the support of high-ranking military commanders and the major industrial leaders, Hitler's power was secure.

It did not take Hitler long to demonstrate his ruthless pursuit of complete power. As soon as he declared his Nazi slogan of "One People, One Government, One Leader," it became apparent that civil rights and democratic institutions in Germany were doomed. First, Hitler banned public demonstrations. Then, he put his close follower Heinrich Himmler in complete charge of the police as well as the Gestapo, the secret Nazi police force notorious for its terror tactics. Himmler and the Gestapo beat, tortured, and jailed thousands of Germans who opposed Hitler. Even long-standing friends who had done much to help Hitler rise to power were eliminated. For instance, Ernest Roehm, leader of the storm troopers, was executed along with one thousand others who dared to disagree with the Führer, or grand leader, as Hitler now called himself. This bloody purge took place on June 30, 1934.

Germany rearms itself

Despite the fact that the Treaty of Versailles prohibited Germany from rearming itself, Hitler convinced the industrial leaders that the best way to overcome the country's economic depression was to manufacture more products, especially weapons. Hitler made the owners of the country's big factories believe that it was more honorable to rebuild Germany's devastated economy than to abide by a treaty forced upon them by foreign enemies.

With the defense industries back in business, hundreds of thousands of young Germans entered the military services to be trained in the latest methods of warfare. German women were to serve their country by having many Aryan babies, and rewards were given to those who gave birth

Hitler employed a propaganda minister, Joseph Goebbels, to organize campaigns to promote Nazism. Goebbels skillfully used the mass media to intensify persecution of the Jews.

most frequently. School teachers had to teach Nazi principles, and eight million boys and girls between the ages of ten and eighteen were ordered to join the Hitler Youth movement. They were encouraged to spy on their own parents and report on the anti-Nazi views of their teachers. Wearing a swastika arm band, each youth was required to greet others with a stiff arm salute, accompanied by the customary uttering of "Heil Hitler!" (Hail Hitler).

Germans gather around a sign that reads, "The Jews are our misfortune." Similar anti-Semitic signs appeared throughout Nazi Germany.

Nazi propaganda

Hitler realized the value of using propaganda to promote his master race theory as well as to discredit other ideas and doctrines he did not like. His propaganda minister, Joseph Goebbels, relied on deception, distortions, and falsehoods to brainwash people into accepting Nazi claims of superiority. The German press, radio, and film studios were taken over and all forms of communication were censored so that no one could publicly criticize the Nazis. The German life-style and culture were represented as being superior to any others, especially to that of the Jews. But German Jews were an integral part of German life.

Most of the Jews in Germany had entered the mainstream of German culture and flourished as members of the middle and upper-middle class. Many Jews were successful merchants and manufacturers and others were doctors, teachers, and scientists.

Goebbels's propaganda machine used the economic success and superior education of many Jews to stir up anti-Jewish envy and hatred. Few who opposed this hatred dared to speak out and challenge the Nazis. Those who did were called Communists, a group that was now in great disfavor. Many Germans, especially younger ones, were excited by the uniforms, military parades,

The Nazis gained much of their power by censoring public information. Here, Nazi officials confiscate armfuls of books considered threatening to the Nazi cause.

and massive patriotic rallies and automatically accepted the anti-Jewish propaganda handed out by the Nazis.

Part of the propaganda campaign was the censorship of literature. Books written by Jewish authors or sympathetic to the Jews as well as other books deemed simply unfit for Nazi readers were snatched from library shelves and publicly burned in huge bonfires. Even the Lutheran clergy, representing Germany's largest single religious group, lost their freedom of speech. Catholic priests and other religious leaders tended to remain silent.

Hitler had planned his strategy well. With the German people fired up for battle against those he deemed the country's enemies—the Jews, the Communists, and the foreigners who had humiliated Germany after World War I—the Führer was ready to begin his bid for world power and to get revenge on the Jews.

2

German
Terrorism

ADOLF HITLER'S PERSECUTION of German Jews turned from words of hate to deeds of destruction early in 1933. Jewish businesses were boycotted and vandalized. Jews were spat upon, stoned, and beaten in the streets. Jewish workers were dismissed from government jobs. Schools and universities were closed to them. Anti-Semitic graffiti appeared throughout Germany. Even the walls of synagogues were defaced with Nazi swastikas and such expressions as "Jew pig," "die Jew," or "when Jewish blood spurts from the knife—then all will be fine."

Humiliation and oppression

Hitler and his Nazis did not stop at mere humiliation and oppression of the Jews. Hitler organized a black-shirted security squad called the *Schutzstaffel*, or SS for short. On their uniforms, they wore the sinister symbols of death—a skull and crossbones. On their arm bands were swastikas. Their daggers displayed a single inscription: "My honor is loyalty." To Hitler they pledged their "obedience until death." Jews were overcome with fear and panic at the approach of SS men, for this could mean immediate arrest without

(opposite page) An anti-Semitic poster urges German citizens not to buy from Jews.

Six-pointed yellow stars brand members of this wedding party as Jews.

ever learning the charges against them. Heinrich Himmler headed the SS. Serving under him were Reinhard Heydrich, in charge of internal spying, and Adolf Eichmann, responsible for Jewish affairs. Both of these men had the fate of millions of Jews in their hands, hands that were eventually to be smeared with Jewish blood.

By 1935, Jews became horrified as they began to see what might be in store for them. Many Jews, especially those who could afford to, left Germany. The overwhelming majority, however, had no relations abroad to receive them, and most of the countries near Germany had closed their borders or had placed strict quotas on immigrants. Those who were fortunate enough to leave left in haste and without money. They were, however, allowed to take personal belongings with them. But countless numbers were forced to leave members of their families, friends, and loved ones behind.

On September 15, 1935, in a series of laws passed in the city of Nuremberg, Jews lost their German citizenship. Jews could no longer marry non-Jews. They could no longer vote. The Nuremberg laws also prohibited Jews from engaging in certain types of work. Jewish doctors could serve only as medical assistants. Newborn Jews were compelled to assume Jewish first names and carry special ID cards imprinted with the letter *J* for the German word for Jew, Jude. Every Jewish male had to take the middle name of Israel. Jewish females were forced to take on the middle name of Sarah to represent their Jewish identity. Not long afterward, Jews were made to wear a six-pointed yellow star with the inscription of "Jude" sewn on their clothes.

Inge Deutchkron, a young Jewish girl, later recalled the day the stars were introduced:

> I looked around me. I saw dozens of people also wearing the star of David—blond men, red-haired women, a white-haired old gentleman with the boldly-etched features of a Viking. All of them Jews; all wearing the yellow badge of shame which was to stamp them pariahs [outcasts]. But we were not pariahs.

In early November 1938, the situation for the German Jews took a turn for the worse. In Paris, a Jewish teenager learned that his father, a Polish Jew living in Germany, was being sent back to Poland, and the son went into a rage and shot a German official at the embassy. It was a shot that was to be heard throughout Europe. Immediately, the Nazi propaganda officials ordered a secret plan of action to take revenge against the Jews.

Reinhard Heydrich salutes the Führer. Heydrich was in charge of internal spying within the SS.

Kristallnacht—"The Night of Broken Glass"

On the nights of November 9 and 10, 1938, while the police stood by, large gangs of Nazi thugs and hoodlums stampeded into Jewish neighborhoods, attacked Jewish people, and destroyed their property. Throughout Germany, Jewish offices, shops, businesses, and private homes were ransacked, looted, and burned by the marauders. Jews were fiercely beaten. Strict observers of the

Members of the SS round up Jews in Vienna. As the Nazi's deadly goals became increasingly apparent, many Jews fled Germany. However, the majority had little money and no relations abroad and were forced to remain in Germany.

Jewish faith who, according to tradition, kept their beards long, were humiliated by having their beards cut as non-Jewish bystanders laughed at them. Many gathered to watch the spectacle. Those who tried to escape were most often shot. Many died, and hundreds were wounded.

More than thirty thousand people were arrested, merely for being Jewish. Historian Alfred Werner was arrested, along with several other Jews, while innocently walking down the street. He described what happened later at the police station:

> At eleven P.M. storm troopers arrived to take charge of us. We were herded into a dark prison van and driven to a Nazi barracks. On our arrival, we had to run the gauntlet of a wild mob who beat us with sticks and iron bars. The first to enter the barracks was shot at once. . . . Three or four persons went mad that night. A boy of eighteen tried to commit suicide by jumping out of a window. . . . The boy had cut one of the arteries of his neck and he died despite the frantic efforts of some doctors in our midst to stop the flow of blood.

The two-day toll of destruction was tremendous. The rioters and terrorists caused millions of dollars' worth of damage. In total, 191 synagogues were burned, and 76 were completely ruined. Fires were allowed to burn while uniformed fire fighters watched. Cemeteries were invaded, and Jewish tombstones were desecrated. The vandalism and bloodbath that took place came to be known as *Kristallnacht* (Crystal Night), or "The Night of Broken Glass," because the streets of so many of Germany's cities were strewn with the broken glass from the windows and storefronts of Jewish homes and businesses. And to cause more pain and suffering, the Nazis ordered the Jews to pay for the damages.

Kristallnacht was the beginning of the end for Germany's Jewish population. In 1933, 600,000 Jews lived in Germany. Many were descendants of Jews who had settled in that country nearly two thousand years earlier. Now they had become victims of a vicious Nazi policy of racism and terror.

Concentration camps

Many of the Jews arrested on Kristallnacht were sent to concentration camps. Concentration camps were Nazi-sponsored prison camps in which political opponents and members of minority groups, particularly Jews, were confined. The first German concentration camp was built at Osthofen near Worms in 1933. Another was then built at Dachau in Germany to imprison those Jews considered to be disloyal to the new order. By 1939, camps existed at Buchenwald, Flossenburg, Mauthausen, Ravensbruck, and Sachsenhausen. These camps began to fill up rapidly with

Jewish passports and other identification cards were imprinted with the letter J for Jude—the German word for Jew.

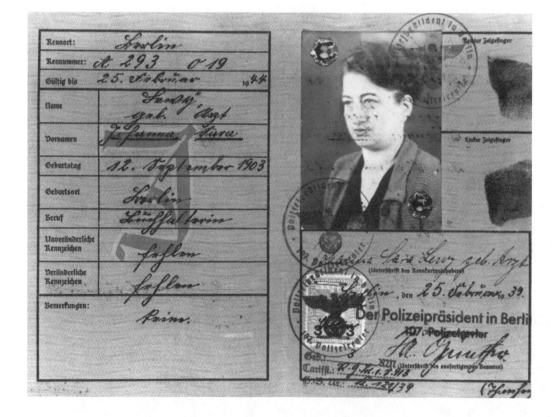

tens of thousands of German Jews who only a few years earlier had been productive citizens of the Reich.

The suffering of the victims began even before they reached the camps. One person who later escaped described how the Nazis loaded 6,000 Jews onto a train bound for the Calarasi concentration camp in Romania:

> Eventually the victims were herded into railway trucks, 100 to 120 people in each. They were not given any food, nor a single drop of water. The heat and stench inside were fearful. . . . There were some who drank their own urine or that of their friends. . . . On the way the victims were robbed of all the clothes that had been left them.

Of the 6,000 people who began the journey, 2,530 died before reaching their destination.

By 1938, Hitler's desire to expand the Reich beyond its borders had become a reality. Having

Jews are searched and arrested on a Berlin street.

Germany dominate other European nations was always his intention. In March of that year, the German army marched unopposed into Austria. There, too, the Jewish population was immediately persecuted and degraded. Jewish men and women of Vienna, even the elderly, were forced to scrub the streets on their hands and knees, while Austrians sympathetic to the Nazis cheered. Jewish shops were looted of their merchandise, and Jewish property was seized. Many Jews and other Austrians were arrested. When Adolf Eichmann was appointed head of Jewish affairs in Austria, it became apparent that the fate of the Jews in that country would soon be as hopeless as that of their fellow Jews in Germany.

Residents of Austria cheer as German troops march into the country. For the Austrian Jews, this advance heralded the onslaught of persecution and loss of rights.

3

Life and Death in the Ghettos of Eastern Europe

BY JANUARY 1939, the plight of the Jews in Germany was alarming. Hitler decreed that all shops, industries, and businesses throughout the country could be owned only by Aryans. This enabled the government to take over all Jewish property. But the most ominous threat came when Hitler predicted that if war were to start with countries unfriendly to Germany, Germany would exterminate the Jewish race in Europe.

Germany invades its neighbors

On March 15, German troops moved into and occupied Czechoslovakia without opposition from other nations. Almost immediately, the younger and stronger Czech Jews were sent to slave-labor concentration camps in Germany. They were forced to work in dangerous ammunition factories and to help build Nazi war machinery. Older Jews, weaker men, women, and children were deported to Poland in the months that followed.

On September 1, 1939, German tanks and infantry troops moved into Poland. Since England

(opposite page) Workers build a ten-foot-high wall to seal off movement to and from the Warsaw ghetto. The Nazis packed thousands of Jews into overcrowded ghettos, where many died of starvation and disease.

35

In Czechoslovakia, a woman weeps as she dutifully salutes Hitler. She is just one of silent millions forced to support Nazism.

This 1941 photograph illustrates the ruthless tactics used by the Einsatzgruppen, *or mobile killing units.*

and France had treaties with Poland that guaranteed their help in defending it, both of these countries declared war on Germany and launched World War II. Poland, however, was forced to surrender in less than one month's time. Its army was overwhelmed by the Nazi use of a new type of warfare called the blitzkrieg, which is a sudden, swift, large-scale attack designed to win a quick victory before the enemy's defenses can be organized.

The Jewish population of Poland numbered 3,250,000 at the time of the German invasion. Jews had lived in Poland for 850 years. Immediately after conquering Poland, the Nazi leaders put into action the "final solution of the Jewish problem," which really meant exterminating the Jews.

At first, the officers of the *Einsatzgruppen,* the

mobile units of the security police and SS that followed the German armies, sought out Jews to shoot. A typical mass execution took place in Lomazy in Poland in August 1942. It was described later during the trial of one of the Nazi officers involved:

> About 1,600-1,700 Jews lived in Lomazy in August 1942 . . . the reserve police battalion . . . surrounded the Jewish living quarter in the early morning hours. . . . The Jews were assembled on the sports grounds . . . the children and elderly, the sick and weak, who were not able to walk, were shot on the spot . . . a working group of fifty Jews . . . had to dig a large pit . . . Jews were taken to the execution place by groups. . . . The Jews had to undress right before the shootings and hand over their valuables . . . [they] had to lie in the pits face down, and then they were shot. The next group of victims had to lie down in a row behind those who had already been killed or on top of them, and then they, too, were shot. The executions continued in that way until the pit . . . was filled to the edge with corpses.

Later, Nazi leaders realized it would be more efficient if the victims were brought to the killers. At least one million Jews were killed by the SS assassination squads, but now the Nazis were eager to destroy all the Jews as quickly as possible. It seemed that the process of herding groups of defenseless Jews onto remote farms, stripping off their clothing, and machine-gunning them to death was too time-consuming. A more efficient plan was needed. First, the Nazis gathered together the Jews living in small communities and the many Jews who had fled to Poland from other countries and transported them to the crowded Jewish ghettos of the cities. The Polish cities were crowded with large numbers of Jews living in the ghettos. It was fairly common for the Jews of eastern European cities to be forced to live within their own ghettos. Inside the restricted

Members of the Einsatzgruppen *pose for the camera in the fall of 1941.*

ghetto, they were forced by the Nazis to work as slave laborers. In a way, the ghetto was much like a walled-off city and similar to a large prison. Since many Jews in occupied Poland were skilled tailors, they were compelled to sew uniforms for the German army. Those who were strong and physically able were pressed into doing hard work in the fields or on the roads, or they were assigned to railroad track battalions. If they were unable to work, they were given no food.

In time, only those who were fit and healthy managed to survive the harsh, cramped conditions in the ghettos of Warsaw, Lodz, Krakow, Lublin, Lvov, and other Polish cities. The Nazis never planned to keep the Jews in the ghettos permanently. It was only a temporary measure until all the cities of Europe could be "cleansed" of Jews, as the Nazi chiefs described the Jews' ultimate fate. But as long as they were confined in the ghettos, life for them was a nightmare.

Ghetto conditions

Once the Nazis had forced the Jews into the mostly walled-off ghettos, they tried to trick their Jewish prisoners into cooperating. They set up a Jewish council, called *Judenrat*, in which the Jews were supposedly given control of their own internal affairs. In that way, the Jews were led to believe that they would be in control of their destiny. But in reality, they had no power and were forced to carry out German orders and commands.

As more and more Jews were packed into ghetto areas of four or five blocks in slumlike tenement apartments, living conditions deteriorated. Existence in these extremely crowded surroundings was becoming intolerable.

Soon after the fall of Poland, many more Jews were forced to live in the ghettos. Sometimes, tens

The Nazis formed the Judenrat, *or Jewish council, as a ploy to delude Jews into thinking they had some control over their destiny.*

of thousands would arrive at one ghetto in a day. The Lodz ghetto, already isolated from the outside world, had 165,000 inhabitants. It was formed in 1940. The Warsaw ghetto, which was the largest, contained 450,000 Jews. The ghettos were closed off by barbed wire or wooden fences and were patrolled by German guards who constantly brutalized innocent people. Recalled Alexander Donat, a resident of the Warsaw ghetto:

A Jewish policeman patrols a ghetto street.

> In addition to the normal Nazi beatings and commands to do arduous gymnastics or to lie in the mud, selected victims were ordered to pick up a heavy brick in one hand and a hollow one in the other. When they'd done so, they were ordered to bend forward and because of the imbalance of weights, they invariably fell down, which provided another pretext [reason] for beating them.

The Nazis also set up special Jewish police forces to guard the ghettos for them.

Masses of people wandered around in the

crowded streets of the ghetto. Everyone, from toddlers to their great-grandparents, carried their possessions, usually luggage, clothing, and blankets. Some pushed meager belongings along in carts. Many were homeless or were orphans cared for by strangers.

Inside the ghetto, the Nazi authorities created an environment that resembled a giant prison. Their goal was to cause an eventual physical and mental breakdown of the captive Jews to ensure that they were not strong enough to rebel. Many were forced to live in hallways, under bridges, in piles of trash, or anywhere they would be protected from the rain, snow, or cold. The unhygienic conditions were horrifying. Sometimes, more than fifteen people were forced to live together in one room. Plumbing frequently broke down, and bathing became difficult. Toilets could not be flushed. People often slept on the floor or on kitchen tables. Many wells were polluted, and the available water was unfit to drink. Fresh air was rare, and epidemics became frequent. Cholera, typhus, and tuberculosis spread rapidly. In 1940 in the Warsaw ghetto, a typhoid fever outbreak took the lives of more than fifteen thousand people within less than one month.

Battling starvation

As difficult as it was for the ghetto inhabitants to avoid sickness, especially since it was almost impossible to obtain medicine, it was even more difficult for them to avoid starvation. The only food available in the ghetto was whatever the Nazis rationed. Some days, nothing was provided. Consuming enough calories to enable the Jews to do hard work was impossible. A typical food allowance was between one-half and two-thirds of the minimum daily calorie requirement. And the nutritional value of the rations was extremely low. Much of the food was rotten.

Jan Karski, a member of the Polish underground, remembered seeing a crowd of Jews in the Warsaw ghetto:

> Mothers huddled close together on benches nursing withered infants. Children, every bone in their skeletons showing through their taut skins, played in heaps and swarms. "They play before they die," I heard my companion . . . say, his voice breaking with emotion.

Most of the time, the Jews received their meals from communal soup kitchens. Potato broth, stale black bread, and fat were offered each day. Soon, the men, women, and children of the ghetto became emaciated.

The refugees, aware that they might soon starve to death, pleaded for food. Many risked

A homeless family huddles on a ghetto street. In addition to the problem of keeping warm, ghetto dwellers constantly fought hunger, illness, and disease.

Desperate for food, crowds gather at a ghetto marketplace.

instant death by smuggling food into the ghetto from the other side of the wall in exchange for money and clothing they had hidden from the Nazi SS troops. Such exchanges could prolong their lives and the lives of their loved ones if they were not caught.

Polish Christians living outside the ghetto wall were given a larger food allotment. Some were willing to swap food for valuables. Others were willing to give food to the Jews. The Jews traveled back and forth through secret underground tunnels or through sewers that led to their non-Jewish neighbors. The more daring, those operating above ground, would loosen bricks in the wall. They could get out by removing the bricks and replacing them upon their return. Because they were smaller and quicker than adults, many children became adept at smuggling.

Some Jews in closely guarded work gangs were

allowed to work outside the ghetto. A few drove carts loaded with human waste and garbage beyond the walls. The return trips afforded them opportunities to smuggle small quantities of food or other items past the watchful eyes of the sentries. But food smuggling helped very little in the struggle against starvation for most of the ghetto Jews.

Struggle for survival

In addition to the problems of finding shelter and food, keeping clean, and overcoming illness and disease, the ghetto dwellers needed to keep warm. The severe shortage of fuel compounded their misery, particularly during the bitterly cold winters. The search for wood to burn as fuel in kitchen stoves, bakery ovens, and in public buildings became desperate. Obtaining coal was almost impossible. The Nazis had confiscated much of the warm clothing. People had little choice except to use whatever wood was available. Household furniture and wood trim in the apartments as well as doors, door frames, and parts of buildings were torn apart for burning. In the Lodz ghetto during the excessively cold winter of 1940 and 1941, fuel riots broke out. And hundreds froze to death.

As one might expect, there was envy, disagreement, and even fighting among some of the ghetto inhabitants. The Nazis sometimes granted special benefits and considerations to certain individuals. Opportunities for obtaining a slightly better existence came to those who had skills that were in demand by the Nazis or to those who were picked to do labor outside the ghetto. Their meals on the job were somewhat better, and some Jews were even in a position to perform favors for Germans and receive favors in return. The original ghetto residents could often stay in their own apartments, despite the fact that they were forced to take in newcomers from the countryside or from other countries. Their situation was better than that of the recent arrivals because they had stored food to be used in emergencies. Those who were able to hide cash, jewels, and valuable household items could arrange with a network of secret traders to barter or sell their goods to Polish Christians in exchange for food. Many forms of bribery were practiced as well, especially for the purpose of getting food, a better job, or a more livable apartment. People were determined to survive, almost at any cost. They would do practically anything to remain alive.

As the months of living in the ghetto caused increased distress, Jews began to criticize the practices and policies that were made by the *Judenrat*. Some members were even suspected of cooperating with the Nazis to gain privileges for themselves. The Jews especially resented the Jewish police and called some of them traitors. The Polish police were hated for their role in driving the Jews out of their provincial towns, where they were brutalized and then robbed of everything they owned. But most of the fear and contempt was directed toward the Nazi SS guards who resorted to whips, guns, and even public executions as a means of keeping the Jewish inmates in line.

Maintaining morale

Despite the constant struggle for survival in the oppressive ghetto environment, the Jews made an almost unbelievable effort to maintain their morale and preserve their sanity. Though isolated from the outside world, they kept informed about current events by listening to the few outlawed radios at their disposal. They were not allowed to pray in their synagogues, so they held small prayer services in their apartments.

Those who were able kept active in neighborhood and community organizations that helped children in orphanages and day-care centers. They did what they could to provide clothing, food, and medicine for the sick, the elderly, and the destitute. Some sponsored lectures, Yiddish theaters, poetry recitals, and concerts.

In the Warsaw ghetto, the Jews published underground newspapers until writers and distributors were found out, arrested, and executed on April 18, 1942.

Providing for the education of children, which has traditionally been an important priority of the Jewish people, became an even greater priority in the ghetto. Schools were established to provide all levels of instruction, with much attention given to vocational training. Though there were enormous problems in getting schoolbooks,

Because the Nazis outlawed all Jewish religious activities, the Jews conducted many of their services behind closed doors. Here, a group of elderly men risks death by holding a clandestine prayer service in the Warsaw ghetto.

supplies, desks, chairs, and classroom space, education prevailed in the ghetto. What was especially amazing was that most of the classes had to meet in secret because normal schooling was usually forbidden. Children who were too sick to attend these secret classes were allowed to borrow books from clandestine libraries. Rachel Auerbach remembered how important books from these libraries were to sick children living in quarantined shelters:

> In the shelters, the children lived in horrible conditions. . . . They had no shoes and clothing and there was no fuel to heat these places in the winter. Yet these children also borrowed and read books. . . . They would reach for the precious gift of books . . . with outstretched, emaciated arms. . . . The children would huddle under one blanket and listen rapturously to an adventure story that took place somewhere under blue skies in the sunny lands of Asia or Africa.

Atrocities

The inhuman oppression of Jews in the Warsaw ghetto lasted from October 1940 until its destruction in June 1943. An array of diaries, belongings, and photographs found in the archives of Yad Vashem, the Martyrs' and Heroes' Remembrance Museum in Jerusalem, Israel, attests to the suffering of the Jews in the Polish ghettos.

Pictures on display in the museum show starving children and adults begging for money to obtain a morsel of food. Some photos are of crowded streets with people lying flat and helpless on the ground, too weak to move. A few are of lame, crippled, and blind people. Others are of people missing an arm or leg; all too frequently, these injuries and disabilities were the result of beatings by Nazi SS police. Forlorn street vendors are seen selling small items, like combs, shoelaces, and postcards. Some photos show women offering handmade Star of David arm bands, required to be worn by all ghetto Jews.

Some photographs portray great numbers of near-naked children, left parentless, sitting or sleeping on rags. Pictures of entire families, dead in their apartments, gnawed on for weeks by rats, are also on exhibit. There are also the snapshots of people carrying the lifeless remains of fellow Jews to common graves in carts, bicycle rickshaws, and improvised stretchers.

Some eighty-five thousand Jews died in the Warsaw ghetto. More than twenty thousand were children. In the three summer months of 1941, nearly sixteen thousand people died of hunger and sickness. Many more thousands died in the other Polish ghettos of similar causes, while untold numbers died by execution. Moreover, the Nazi policy of forcing Jewish boys and men to work nonstop, from sunup to sundown, in slave-labor battalions contributed to the death toll. Some died trying to escape the closely guarded work assignments. Others died from whippings when they could no longer find the stamina to do the physically demanding and brutal work.

The frightening ghetto experience was slowly destroying the Jews. But for the Nazis, the pace of annihilation was still too slow. Plans for another, quicker, more devastating method of killing the remaining Jews were being put in place.

Members of the SS search Warsaw Jews for hidden weapons.

4

Deportations to Concentration Camps

ON JUNE 22, 1941, Hitler's armed forces, called the *Wehrmacht*, invaded the western part of the Soviet Union, despite a nonaggression pact that had been signed by the two countries in 1939. It became increasingly apparent that the German dictator was determined to capture all of Europe with his powerful armies. Germany had already taken over Austria, and its troops occupied Czechoslovakia. Great Britain and France declared war on Germany on September 3, 1939, but failed to stop the German invasion of Denmark, Norway, the Netherlands, Belgium, or Luxembourg. It did not take long for the Baltic Sea countries of Lithuania, Estonia, and Latvia, along with Greece, the Balkan nations, and the rest of eastern Europe, to succumb to Hitler's might. Two countries, Italy and Japan, joined Germany to form the Axis powers in 1940.

(opposite page) These emaciated men are liberated inmates of Lager Nordhausen, a concentration camp where inmates were brutally beaten and starved to death.

Mobile killing units

By 1942, millions of Jews throughout Europe were being rounded up and deported to concentration camps. Their nationality made no difference

49

German forces invade the Soviet Union. This invasion led many to question Hitler's aggressive, expansionist goals.

to the *Einsatzgruppen*, or mobile killing units, whose duty was to massacre Jews in the cities and towns of the newly captured countries. It was not uncommon for some local people to reveal Jewish hiding places to the Nazis or to turn in Jews when they tried to pass themselves off as Christians. These collaborators were especially helpful to the Germans in the Soviet republics of Belorussia and the Ukraine and in the Baltic territories.

When the *Einsatzgruppen* arrived in a town, the Germans generally and immediately rounded up its Jewish population. Told that they were about to be resettled, the Jews were marched off to the outskirts of the city or into a wooded area at gunpoint. Once assembled at a secluded spot, the Jews were forced to undress in front of a huge pit and then were shot down in groups. Hundreds of thousands were executed in this manner and buried in mass graves where they fell dead. One of the few survivors was Rivka Yosselevska, a young mother from Pinsk in the Soviet Ukraine. Her child was ripped from her arms, shot, and then she too was shot. She recounted:

> Then I fell to the ground into the pit amongst the bodies. . . . Then I felt that I was choking; people falling all over me. . . . I felt bodies pulling at me with their hands, biting at my legs, pulling me down, down.

When the Germans were gone, she managed to crawl from the pit and recover from her wounds.

Adolf Eichmann, one of the top Nazi officials in charge of killing Jews, admitted at his postwar trial that he had witnessed storm troopers shooting at a pit full of moving bodies. "I can still see," said Eichmann, "a woman with a child. She was shot and then the baby in her arms. His brains splattered all around, also over my leather overcoat."

The clothes that the Jewish victims were ordered to shed were washed and sent back to the Reich for Germans to wear.

Some of the executioners were quite sadistic;

German soldiers round up prisoners.

German Jews gather their belongings during deportation to a concentration camp.

they took pleasure in killing their victims. Others did not feel good about having to shoot women and children but seemed to enjoy murdering Jewish men. To avoid the executioners' aversion to murdering women and children, another system for large-scale destruction was employed. Jews were led into large vans and told they were going to enjoy a much-needed shower. As soon as ninety to one hundred entered the van, guards closed the doors and piped in exhaust fumes from the engine, causing death by asphyxiation, or lack of oxygen.

Einsatzgruppen officers trying to impress Heinrich Himmler, commander of the SS, and other high-ranking officials in Berlin, began to increase their killing of Jews. Nearly 800,000 Soviet Jews were savagely murdered by the *Einsatzgruppen*. In the Soviet city of Odessa, 19,000 Jews were murdered. In the largest single massacre of the war, some 35,000 Jews were killed in only two days of shooting at a ravine at Babi Yar, near Kiev, the capital of the Ukraine.

The "final solution" draws nearer

On December 8, 1941, one day after Japan bombed Pearl Harbor, which brought the United States into the war, the Chelmno extermination camp near the city of Lodz, Poland, went into operation. Seven hundred Jews were gassed in a mobile van, and the annihilation of Europe's Jews seemed to be progressing. Shortly thereafter, Himmler moved quickly to remove the Jews from the ghettos, cities, towns, and villages in Germany and the conquered lands. At a special meeting of Nazi leaders, called the Wannsee Conference, held outside Berlin, it was decided that eleven million Jews were to be killed. Those able to work would be the last to be exterminated. In the minds of the Nazis, this plan would be the "final solution" of the Jewish problem. As Adolf Eichmann coldly declared, "Jewry is now suffering a fate which, though hard, is more than deserved. No compassion and certainly no sorrow is called for. In this historic conflict every Jew is our enemy."

Adolf Hitler and Heinrich Himmler liked the idea of setting up extermination camps to gas vast numbers of Jews. At the Wannsee session, Reinhard Heydrich, the heartless SS leader, and SS Col. Adolf Eichmann were placed in charge of carrying out the total destruction of the European Jewry. Eichmann was put in charge of the "Jewish section" of the Gestapo. In May 1942, however, Heydrich was assassinated by Czech partisans, or secret guerrilla fighters, who were parachuted into Czechoslovakia by the British Air Force. Angered by the assassination, the Nazis wiped out the entire male population of Lidice, a Czech mining village of 450 people.

At the Wannsee Conference, the Nazis decided that anyone having "impure" blood, such as the child of a Jewish-Aryan marriage or even a child who had a Jewish grandparent, was a dangerous enemy. These people, too, were sent to the concentration camps and put to death, even if they were practicing Christians.

The Nazis were experienced in killing children. In 1939, they had begun a program of "mercy killing" German children who were physically or mentally handicapped. Unable to fit the Nazi image of a master race, these children were injected with fatal doses of poison. People with incurable diseases or mental disorders were put to death in a similar fashion. Also, tens of thousands of Jews, Gypsies, political enemies, some war prisoners, and "inferior" people of all nationali-

Nazi commanders used pellets of Zyklon B in the gas chambers of the death camps.

ties were murdered. At that point, the Nazi death camp commanders began to use deadly gas pellets of a substance called Zyklon B. Rudolf Hess, the commander at Auschwitz, described the first use of the new gas:

> In the crowded cells, death came instantaneously the moment the Zyklon B was thrown in. A short, almost smothered cry, and it was all over. . . . I must admit that this gassing set my mind at rest, for the mass extermination of the Jews was to start soon. . . . Now, we had the gas, and we had established a procedure.

Killing centers using gas chambers were built in early 1942 after the Nazis learned that large numbers of people could be killed quickly and with the help of few personnel. The expansion program of building more gas chambers and then burning the bodies in ovens, or crematories, was known as Operation Reinhard. The method was named after the unmerciful Reinhard Heydrich, chief planner of the mass executions.

Concentration camps and extermination camps

Concentration camps became collection points for Jews and others before their transportation to the extermination camps. A number of concentration camps were also turned into death factories. The most infamous extermination camp was Auschwitz, also called Auschwitz-Birkenau, in southern Poland. The names of other large camps that specialized in death by gassing, like Belzec, Sobibor, and Treblinka in eastern Poland, along with Chelmno in western Poland, will be remembered as symbols of human cruelty forever. At other concentration or death camps like Mauthausen in Austria; Maidanek in Poland; and Dachau, Bergen-Belsen, Buchenwald, and Sachsenhausen, all on German soil, thousands more lost their lives. They are sites where some of the most horrible atrocities in the history of the world

This 1945 photograph documents how starved prisoners died enroute to the Dachau concentration camp.

were committed.

Most concentration camps were built to serve similar purposes. They were designed as huge enclosures to house working prisoners. Five of the camps were used for the immediate killing of entire trainloads of new arrivals. Mauthausen was a camp for men. Ravensbruck, north of Berlin, was a women's camp. In Bohemia, the Nazis established a so-called "model" ghettolike garrison camp at Theresienstadt. Theresienstadt was really a decoy to convince the outside world that concentration camp living was not so bad. It was designed for communal living. It had dormitories and even provided opportunities for inmates to participate in cultural activities. Meat and vegetables were served. As a result, when foreign visitors from the International Red Cross came to inspect a "typical" concentration camp, they were easily deceived. They were led to believe that the rumors being circulated about horrible conditions at the concentration camps were untrue. They failed to realize that although conditions at Theresienstadt were better than at other concentration camps, it was still a temporary station on the road to the extermination camps.

By the summer of 1942, Himmler had ordered all Polish ghettos closed and had given the SS six months to deport the remaining ghetto Jews to the camps. Approximately seven or eight thousand were to be deported each day. Skilled workers and their families needed to perform jobs in German factories had the best chance of not being sent to the camps. Children, women, and old people were the first to be rounded up. The Germans often attempted to prevent the Jews from panicking by telling them that they were merely being resettled in another location where they would have food and be able to work. Some Jews even received mailed postcards from friends and relatives previously taken away, saying they were well. But many of the Jews were highly suspi-

Polish children were photographed and numbered upon arrival to Auschwitz-Birkenau.

Prisoners peer from a railroad car during their deportation to Auschwitz-Birkenau in 1944.

cious of this trick and feared the worst. Even when they were told that they could take a few pounds of personal belongings with them, including valuables and enough food to last three days, they mistrusted the Nazis.

When the time came to leave, they were marched to a large building next to a railroad station. All were extremely frightened. Anyone found hiding or lagging behind would be shot by the SS. Perhaps the most pathetic sight of all was to see little, ill-clothed children with their hands raised in a sign of surrender. They were being forced into the lines at gunpoint or by the barking and biting of trained police dogs.

The Jews were shoved into converted boxcars or makeshift cattle cars. Each car usually had two or three small windows covered with barbed wire. As many as sixty to one hundred people were jammed into a car, which was bolted from the outside. The foul odor and stifling air in the almost completely closed cars brought much misery and suffering to the occupants. The three-to-ten-day train ride to the camps was extremely dehumanizing. It was not uncommon for sickness to spread or for people to die en route. There was little food and water and no toilet facilities. Two buckets were provided, one for drinking water and one for the passengers to urinate into. Occasionally, a more understanding train commander would allow those on board to get out of the cars for a quick rest stop along the track embankment.

Mass deportations

By the summer of 1942, Jews from Belgium, Croatia, France, the Netherlands, and Poland had been deported to extermination camps. By October of that year, all Jews in German concentration camps were ordered deported to Auschwitz. In the winter of 1942, Jews from Greece and Norway were sent away to the camps. In March 1943, new crematories were opened in Auschwitz. That month the trainloads of Jews to the "last stop" on the line began to increase by the thousands. These shipments became known as "transports of death." By June 1943, Himmler ordered the destruction of all ghettos in Poland and the Soviet Union. The large ghettos in the Soviet cities of Minsk, Vilna, and Riga were closed down by the fall of 1943. Even a few hundred Danish Jews were expelled from their country at that time. In 1944, trains from Italy also left for the camps.

Hitler's plan was nearing its logical conclusion, the one he had referred to in a speech on January 30, 1939. "During the time of my struggle for power," said Hitler, "I said that I would one day take over the leadership of the state, and with it that of the whole nation, and that I would then among other things settle the Jewish problem." The end result, declared the Führer, would be "the annihilation of the Jewish race in Europe!"

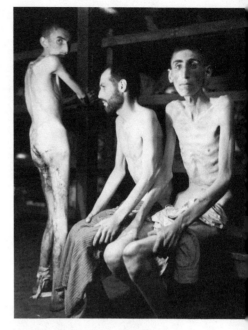

These inmates were healthy and robust when they entered the Buchenwald camp eleven months ago. Now, they are nearly dead from hunger.

5

Barbed Wires and Camp Fires

THE CONCENTRATION CAMPS were death factories. Whether they were camps in which Jews and non-Jews were put to forced labor or those operated solely for the murder of Jews, a stay there was shocking and frightful. Brutality, abuse, starvation, torture, and massacre were common practices in each of the camps. And diseases were widespread throughout the camps as well.

Auschwitz, once a fortress, was also called Auschwitz-Birkenau and was the largest Nazi-operated camp anywhere. It was situated thirty-two miles west of the city of Krakow in southern Poland. The camp covered about fifteen square miles and it consisted of three main camps and thirty-nine lesser camps. About 400,000 prisoners, two-thirds of whom were Jews, were registered in the camp. It is estimated that more than one million people were exterminated there. The Soviets claimed that four times that number died in Auschwitz.

The camp consisted of a complex of buildings resembling long army barracks. They were surrounded by barbed wire and guarded by men stationed in watchtowers.

(opposite page) At the gate of the Theresienstadt camp in Germany, a sign promises inmates that "work makes one free."

The Nazis' system of mass murder was executed with deadly efficiency in the killing centers. To dispose of the bodies—and destroy evidence of the murders taking place—the Nazis burned thousands of corpses in vast crematoriums.

When prisoners arrived at Auschwitz, they saw a big sign over the main gate. It read, *"Arbeit macht frei"* (work makes one free). This was another cruel hoax played on the new inmates; the sign was used to make the Jews think that through hard work they had a chance of living.

At the gateway to the camps, a Nazi doctor or senior SS officer decided which Jews should live to perform slave labor and which should die. This man was responsible for the destinies of thousands of humans. Upon looking over the new arrivals, he pointed to the right or to the left. The healthy-looking men, or even undersized boys who could stretch their bodies erect, would be motioned to the left. Most of the women, the children, and the sickly went to the right. Those sent to the right were doomed to die.

Another Nazi who was in a position to make decisions concerning the new arrivals at Auschwitz was the chief doctor of the camp, Josef Mengele. Though well-mannered and cultured, he defied the laws of decency and morality by conducting horrifying experiments in his special medical laboratory. Mengele selected certain individuals, including twins and dwarfs, and performed gruesome medical tests on them. He claimed these tests were conducted in the pursuit of scientific knowledge. His underlying objective was to find ways to heighten the Aryan characteristics of the German people. Prisoners were deliberately infected with deadly diseases so that new drugs could be tested on them. Painful sterilization procedures were performed on men and women. Dye was injected into brown-eyed people in an effort to turn their eyes blue, which was an Aryan trait. All such experiments on the human guinea pigs led to eventual death of the subjects. Many went mad before they died.

Inhuman treatment in the camps

Dr. Miklos Nyiszli, a Jewish doctor forced to assist Mengele, was ordered to dissect the bodies of many sets of twin children in an attempt to find out if their internal organs were as identical as their faces. Nyiszli assumed that the children had died of natural causes until one day he noticed a small red spot caused by a hypodermic needle. He recalled:

> I was struck by the characteristic odor of chloroform. The victim had received an injection of chloroform in the heart . . . [causing] instantaneous death by heart failure. My discovery of the most monstrous secret of the Third Reich's medical science made my knees tremble. Not only did they kill with gas, but also with injections of chloroform into the heart. A cold sweat broke out on my forehead . . . a shudder of fear ran through me. If Dr. Mengele had any idea that I had discovered the secret . . . he would send ten doctors . . . to attest to my death.

Fearing for his own life, Nyiszli kept quiet about what he had found.

Few survived the harsh conditions of concentration camp life. If prisoners were not gassed or shot, they were starved or worked to death.

Men and women selected for forced labor worked in the mines, factories, or on construction projects located a few miles from their concentration camps. They were forced to march to and from the job site. Inmates worked at least sixteen hours a day and had to produce their daily output quotas or be beaten. Others were responsible for doing all kinds of work within the camps. Almost immediately after their arrival, inmates had blue identification numbers tattooed on their forearms. All of their hair was shaved off. Then, they were outfitted with striped uniforms—the same clothes that were worn for working and sleeping. Sometimes the camp identification numbers were sewn

Starved prisoners pose at a concentration camp in Ebensee, Austria. Prisoners of this camp were used in "scientific" experiments.

onto their outer garments. A prisoner's arrest classification appeared under the number in the form of a color-coded triangle. Political prisoners had red triangles, criminals had green. Black was reserved for the lower classes and Gypsies; pink was born by homosexuals; and Jehovah's Witnesses displayed the color purple. Inmates who had the authority to perform official duties wore arm bands that were variously colored to correspond to their authority level.

Each of the camps usually had six departments. The *Kommandantur*, or commander, of the camp was most often a high-ranking military officer and oversaw the operation of the entire camp. Other sections included the administration, the medical department, the political department where records were kept, the guard troops, and the *Schutzhaftlager*, which was responsible for watching over prisoner barracks and labor brigades. Men and women lived apart in separate barracks. It was not unusual for a husband and wife or close relatives and friends to be housed in barracks only yards away without knowing the whereabouts of each other. As many as eight hundred people would be crowded into a single barracks, sleeping in narrow rows of three-tiered bunks spaced eighteen inches apart. Each bed had a wafer-thin straw mat. During the summer months the damp buildings were infested with flies and insects.

A six-year-old orphan stands for roll call at the Buchenwald camp. Children—and even babies—were not spared from Nazi atrocities.

A harsh existence

Inmates also contended with lice and other vermin. The poorly ventilated barracks reeked with a nauseating stench. Keeping warm in winter was practically impossible. Dirt and mud were ever-present. When water was available, buckets were provided for drinking and for washing. Latrine facilities were primitive. Large barrels and trenches were located in an outside building, and inmates

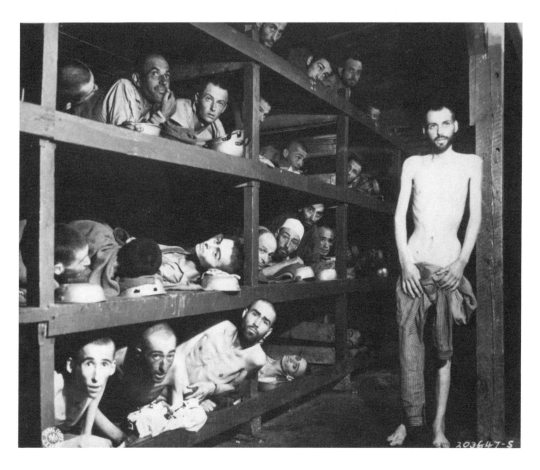

Prisoners peer from their bunks at Buchenwald.

used them at scheduled times or by special permission.

The Nazis supplied little food to the prisoners. Usually, it consisted of watery cabbage soup and sometimes some potatoes and bread. One survivor of the camp at Treblinka remembered:

> From day to day our meager rations were reduced . . . they distributed a slice of bread which was for the morning and which we were not allowed to eat until then. As we twisted and turned on our bunks at night, our insides were so empty that we couldn't stop thinking about that slice of bread until we broke off a piece . . . that tasted like clay and smelled like a sick animal. There were those who gobbled up the entire piece . . . in the morning, they could expect harsh punishment.

Inmates often lost fifty pounds within a few months of confinement. They quickly became human skeletons, and few survived for more than three or four months. Some who could not bear the suffering threw their bodies against the electrified barbed wire fence that surrounded the camp complex.

Inmates were beaten for stealing food, even potato peelings. In another form of punishment, inmates were forced to remain at attention in the hot sun or the bitter cold for hours at a time with their tongues sticking out. Sometimes, they had to hold a heavy rock in front of their bodies for long periods. Disobedience was a serious offense, and an entire barracks could be punished as an example if one person misbehaved. If a member of a brigade escaped, an entire work unit would be shot.

Prisoners designated for death in the gas

Although the Nazis reduced their victims to ashes, they failed to destroy all evidence of their existence. This crate of wedding rings serves as testimony to the atrocities committed.

EUROPE 1938-39

● Cities
■ Concentration Camps
(1938-45)

chambers were never told by their Nazi executioners what was about to happen. Yet many correctly guessed their fate. They were told that they were about to enter the showers in order to get clean. In one camp, grass and shrubs were planted around the building in which the gassing took place to provide a pleasant and peaceful atmosphere. And an orchestra of women prisoners played cheerful music. Men were instructed to go to one hall and undress, and women and children went to another. Jewelry, watches, and eyeglasses were taken from them for safekeeping until they finished their showers, or so they were told.

SS Capt. Kurt Gerstein, who was so ashamed of the mass murders and his part in them that he committed suicide at the end of the war, described the actual killing procedure:

> Mothers with babies at their breasts, naked; lots
> of children of all ages, naked too; they hesitate,
> but they enter the gas chambers, most of them,
> without a word . . . chased by the whips of the SS
> men. . . . Many of them said their prayers; others
> ask: "Who will give us water before our death?"
> Within the chambers, the SS press the people
> closely together. . . . Seven hundred to eight hun-
> dred, crushed together on 25 square meters . . . the
> doors are closed. . . . After twenty-eight minutes
> only a few were alive. After thirty-two minutes, all
> were dead. From the other side, Jewish workers
> opened the wooden doors. The dead were still
> standing like stone statues, there having been no
> room for them to fall or bend over. Though dead,
> the families could still be recognized, their hands
> still clasped. . . . The bodies were thrown out blue,
> wet with sweat and urine, the legs covered with
> excrement and menstrual blood. . . . Dentists with
> chisels tore out gold teeth.

The naked corpses were thrown into wooden
handcarts and hurriedly pushed to the crematory
where the bodies were burned in huge furnaces.
The odor of burning skin rose with the smoke
from the oven's chimneys. It could be seen and
smelled throughout the camp and for miles
around. The five Auschwitz-Birkenau gas chambers and ovens operated day and night. In this
manner, as many as nine thousand individuals per
day were reduced to ashes by the Nazis.

6

Resistance, Rebellion, and Revenge

BY FEBRUARY 1943, World War II began to take a new direction. The Soviet army drove the Axis forces from all of eastern Europe and the Balkans during the next two years. The Allies gradually defeated the German armies in western Europe during this period as well. To hide the evidence of their barbaric treatment of the Jews and other "enemies" of the Reich and avoid retaliation, the Germans tried to destroy the death camps. Though the Nazis attempted to destroy the crematories, those few Jews who were still alive were able to tell their liberators what took place. Furthermore, huge mounds of shoes (including baby bootees), clothing, watches, fountain pens, tens of thousands of suitcases, bins of eyeglasses, and large stacks of recently cut human hair served as evidence of what had happened.

When the world learned about the horrendous events in the death camps, many people wondered why the Jews had not offered more resistance to their oppressors. But the Jews had few opportunities to resist. The muzzle of a gun

(opposite page) These women are among the many who resisted their Nazi oppressors during the Warsaw ghetto revolt.

71

aimed at a person's head, the beatings, the torture, and the public hangings carried out by the Germans made almost all who were imprisoned submissive and docile.

Confronted with the overwhelming strength of the German military, victims had little alternative but to comply with the commands given to them. Obeying meant clinging to precious hours of life in the hope that some unforeseen miracle would change their destiny. Perhaps relief would arrive and rescue them from impending death. Resisting or attacking a guard, on the other hand, invariably resulted in death. Not only was the attacker killed but his family and fellow prisoners were also tortured and executed. In Lvov, where Poland borders the Ukraine, 4,500 Jews were wiped out in

Jewish clothing litters the yard of the Dachau concentration camp. Inmates were forced to strip before being sent to the gas chambers.

one incident of revenge. After two prisoners escaped from the Chelmno camp in Poland, testified former prisoner Tovia Blatt, the Germans announced camp-wide punishments at morning roll call:

> Each tenth prisoner in the rows of the roll call would be executed. He [the guard] is approaching my group. I was seized with fear. . . . He is in the row behind me. My God, only not me. . . . The third from me became the victim. After the selection, the doomed were taken to camp III, and we went to work. Afterward we heard shots, and later the clothes of those who had been killed were brought for sorting.

Such reprisals by the Nazis ensured that the captives did not often resist.

Besides the threat of execution, there were a number of other reasons why most Jews failed to fight or resist and instead remained passive, resigned to the inevitable. Though they held life dear, they knew their pain and agony could be relieved by death. Some even welcomed it. The more religious put their fate in God's hands. Also there were those who believed that the Germans were telling the truth when they promised to resettle the Jews and allow them to live out the war in work camps. To some it was inconceivable that a country as civilized as Germany could be part of a mass-murder scheme.

Many Jews thought that in time the Germans would lose the war and they would be saved. This became more of a possibility after the Nazi armies began to suffer heavy losses and defeats in their battles against Soviet troops on the eastern front. The Jews believed that if they persevered, they would be rescued. And embedded in their beliefs were memories of how their Jewish forebears survived century-old pogroms.

Even when they were inclined to resist, many Jews did not because they were too sick and weak.

This artwork from the Holocaust era portrays Jewish life during the Nazi occupation of Europe.

And if they could muster enough strength to organize some plan of attack, they had no access to the necessary guns or weapons.

A commitment to live

Despite their circumstances, most of the Jews still made an effort to defy Nazi authority. They expressed their defiance by studying their religion and maintaining their cultural habits. Some even expressed themselves through poetry and art. The will to survive made them adept at bribery, forgery, theft, and spying. They resorted to smuggling and sabotage when it was safe to do so. Sometimes in a fit of anger or desperation, they would attack Nazi police officers or camp guards.

The boldest and most aggressive of the Jewish rebels were Zionists, those who wanted to escape to Palestine where they could establish their own Jewish country and be rid of persecution once and for all. They located a few guns and smuggled them into the ghettos. They assembled their own machine guns, piece by piece. They filled bottles with gasoline, wrapped them in saturated rags, and inserted a wick. When ignited, this weapon could be used as an antitank grenade. It was called a Molotov cocktail. Then, as they realized that extermination was almost inevitable, more and more Zionists made a commitment to die fighting with dignity and courage. They were dedicated to killing as many Nazis as they could. To them, that was an honorable goal.

Despite the staggering odds against them, individuals and groups of Jews did strike back at the Nazis. In July 1942, the Jews in the small ghetto of Nieswiez, Poland, started an uprising by throwing acid in the faces of Nazi police officers. After firing a crude machine gun on German reinforcements, the Jewish fighters set fire to the ghetto.

The overpowering Germans retaliated by murdering every Jew in the community. Similar actions followed in other ghettos. Secret Jewish rebel units were established in the ghettos of Vilna, Bialystok, and elsewhere. These units attacked the Nazis and wounded many of them. Although most of the Jewish rebels were men, some were teenage girls.

In Krakow, a squad of Jews dressed in stolen SS uniforms managed to hide a bomb in a restaurant situated outside the ghetto. The bomb exploded and killed several Germans. Once again, the SS men struck back by shooting countless ghetto dwellers. At Treblinka, a Jew about to enter the gas chamber threw a hand grenade at the Ukrainian guards. At the same camp, another

Jewish rebel fighters offered resistance against Nazi terrorism.

SS troops gunned down these prisoners after they were caught fleeing a massacre at Seeshaupt, Germany.

Jewish man, despondent after hearing that his wife and daughter died in the chamber, stabbed and killed an SS officer. It was not uncommon for enraged Jews to strike back at those who harmed them. Often, they stole or made knives and hid them until they had an opportunity to strike.

Uprisings

Three uprisings took place in the Treblinka, Sobibor, and Auschwitz-Birkenau concentration camps from the summer of 1943 to the fall of 1944. Each of the insurrections resulted in limited success. Some Jewish inmates did manage to escape, but hundreds more were killed, captured, and hanged.

In one incident, two young boys who were accused of trying to escape were taken to a gallows in the roll call area where all of the inmates had been gathered. Prisoner Oscar Strawczinski later said, "The two boys were hung naked by their feet. The Germans whipped their swinging bodies for about half an hour, until one of the Germans pulled a gun and shot them." Another witness recalled that, as they hung there, the boys bravely called out, "Jews, escape, because death awaits you also. . . . Our fate today is your fate tomorrow."

Despite such punishments, resistance in the camps continued. Fighting back became a way to win at least a moral victory over the Nazis. In addition to killing SS and Ukrainian guards, the Jews burned camp buildings. Following the rebellions at Treblinka and Sobibor, neither camp could function as an extermination center any longer.

In Treblinka, in Poland, the Jewish underground leaders developed a well-planned escape using makeshift weapons and grenades to storm the fences. They were also able to obtain guns and ammunition from the German arsenal by duplicating a key to the arms storehouse. Unfortunately, the plan failed when an SS officer was shot when he discovered that an inmate had some Polish money, which was forbidden. Many Jews and a number of guards were killed in the fighting inside the camp. Some Jews escaped, but German soldiers pursued them into the fields and captured or shot all but about one hundred before they could reach the woods.

Sobibor uprising

Sobibor, in eastern Poland, was located near partisan units, which were the civilian guerrilla fighters who hid in the forests and carried out surprise raids on German troops and installations. For this reason and because of the rising number of German military defeats, the Nazis placed land mines around Sobibor. At the camp, the Jewish rebels dug a tunnel under the fences and mined areas. When the tunnel collapsed in a rainstorm, the rebel commanders changed their strategy. They decided to conduct their escape by killing a

In Gardelegen, Germany, political prisoners met death as they tried to escape from a barn set afire by the Nazis. One hundred prisoners were locked in the barn before the fire was ignited. Twelve escaped.

Prisoners stand dutifully before Nazi guards. The Nazis kept prisoners obedient by threatening to torture or kill fellow inmates if anyone tried to escape.

group of SS men, then taking their weapons and raiding the camp arsenal.

Though the escape plan was initially successful, too many anxious camp prisoners panicked and ran for the fences and gates before the total operation could be put in effect. A bloody battle took place with heavy casualties suffered by the German and Ukrainian guards. The rebels took staggering losses as well. A few hundred Jews fled Sobibor, but most were eventually caught, shot, or killed by the exploding mines. Some of those who managed to get away joined the nearby partisan forces.

Auschwitz uprising

A revolt erupted inside Auschwitz on October 7, 1944. At that time, the German armies were in full retreat. Nevertheless, Adolf Eichmann and his colleagues ordered that the gas chambers at Auschwitz be in full operation twenty-four hours a day. He wanted to accelerate the process of murdering Jews before the Soviets arrived to liberate them. Previously, on July 24, a contingent of Soviet soldiers had advanced to the death camp at Maidanek and freed all of its inmates. Meanwhile, hundreds of thousands of Hungarian Jews, along with trainloads of Greek Jews and Jews from practically every European country, streamed into Auschwitz daily.

The Auschwitz revolt was unusual in that it was started by *Sonderkommandos*, the special units of Jewish inmates who transported dead bodies to the crematories. They were able to plant explosives under the ovens. The dynamite was smuggled out of an ammunition plant by four girls who were working there. The revolt was triggered by blowing up one crematory and damaging another.

SS men killed

During the gun battle that followed, a number of SS men were killed. Said Dr. Nyiszli, a bomb fell at the feet of a group of SS men:

> Seven SS, including the group commander, fell dead or wounded. . . . The SS opened a deadly fire on the rioters, who retreated and took up defensive positions inside the crematorium . . . a tremendous explosion rocked the area, felling those attackers who had moved in close to the building. The crematorium roof blew off, sending a shower of beams and shingles flying in all directions, while smoke and flames billowed skyward.

Many Jews were also killed when they were captured after breaking through the camp fence and trying to flee. None of the participants in the revolt survived. The four girls involved in supplying the materials for the bomb were tortured and hanged without revealing the names of other underground members. A secret final letter that one of the victims wrote before her execution implored others in the camps to "be strong and brave." The martyrs at Auschwitz were able to slow the rate of mass murder only slightly. Yet, as Dr. Nyiszli commented, "It was indeed an historic event . . . 853 prisoners and 70 SS were killed. . . . Number three crematorium burned to the ground. And number four, as a result of damage to its equipment, was rendered useless."

Jagged barbed wire surrounds a camp at Mauthausen, Austria.

As early as January 1942, the more militant factions in the ghettos of Europe began to plead with their fellow Jews to resist the Nazis, even to the last breath. In Vilna, young people placed posters on walls warning that the Lithuanian Jews were being shot, not resettled at the nearby Ponary camp. Their signs appealed to Jews to disobey the Gestapo and "not go as sheep to slaughter." They said that though it was true that they were weak and defenseless, resistance was the only reply to the enemy. A posted notice read, "Brothers! It is better to fall as free fighters than to live by the grace of the murderers."

The Warsaw ghetto revolts

Early in 1942, the Jews made efforts to establish a guerrilla force in Warsaw. Limited contacts were made with the secret Polish underground detachments, which enabled the budding Jewish

A young boy surrenders to Nazi troops in the Warsaw ghetto.

fighting units to obtain a small number of arms. Some weapons, mostly old revolvers, were purchased outside the ghetto at very high prices and smuggled back in at great risk to both buyer and seller. Weapons and parts were also stolen from gun factories and assembled in the ghetto. Hand grenades were made there in secret shops and stored for future battle.

Despite the great difficulties of convincing most ghetto inhabitants that being passive was futile, the young Warsaw ghetto rebel leaders proceeded with their plans to revolt. They believed that though the remaining Jewish community of seventy thousand Jews was still divided on what course of action to take, they could no longer sit back and do nothing. Germans had to be killed.

On January 18, 1943, the Germans surprised the remaining ghetto occupants with a sweeping raid and ordered all the inhabitants they caught to go to the *Umschlagplatz*, which meant "reloading place." It was the square in the Warsaw ghetto where Jews were herded together for deportation to the death camps. The resistance hurriedly put out a leaflet: "Jews! The enemy has moved on to the second phase of your extermination! Do not resign yourself to death! Defend yourselves! Grab an axe, an iron bar, a knife! Let them take you this way, if they can!"

Insurgence

The Warsaw ghetto Jews responded by launching the first civilian armed resistance to the Nazis with four days of bitter fighting. With a mere 143 revolvers, one machine gun, and sparse rounds of ammunition at their disposal, the "people's avengers," as they were called, struck back at the Nazis in guerrilla-type street fighting. Twenty Germans were killed and fifty wounded. More than one thousand Jews were killed during the

Jewish rabbis are rounded up during the Warsaw ghetto destruction.

resistance. The Nazis sent six thousand off to the death camps, but the mood of the ghetto had changed. Jews realized that they too could kill. This knowledge gave them courage to fortify themselves against the Nazis and death itself.

In the next three months, many Warsaw ghetto members organized themselves into the Jewish Fighting Organization. It was set up like a military command post with soldierly orders and duties. It consisted of 650 fighters comprising twenty-two combat groups. Underground caves were dug, and bunkers were built and stocked with enough food to last through a siege. Entire families retreated to the shelters. For the Jews, Warsaw had become an underground city. People stayed off the streets and moved about by way of trenches, ditches, sewers, and below-ground tunnels. Attic walls were cut from house to house to allow undetected passage between them.

The Germans made one last attempt to lure the Jews out of the Warsaw ghetto peacefully. Factory bosses promised the remaining workers that their existing jobs would be transferred to a lovely location near Lublin. But the suspicious Jews turned down the offer with acts of defiance. Jewish workers proceeded to burn trucks and shop machinery. Known informers and a few despised Jewish police officers were shot for collaborating with the Nazis. These Jews had become Nazi ghetto deputies in order to save their own lives. Special platoons of Jewish rebels went out on dangerous night missions to gather food, smuggle arms, and free Jewish prisoners. They set fire to SS warehouses and sabotaged German installations whenever and wherever they could.

In the first days of April 1943, at a time when the Jews were busy preparing for their Passover holiday, an observance that celebrates the deliverance of the ancient Hebrews from slavery in Egypt, the Germans moved in on the ghetto. Heavily armed soldiers were accompanied by tanks, armored cars, and artillery. The ghetto contingents opened fire on the Nazis from ambush positions. Twelve Germans were killed. They retreated but

SS Major Juergen Stroop leads troops during the Warsaw ghetto revolt.

returned shortly with flamethrowers and set fire to ghetto buildings. Jewish fighters inflicted heavy casualties on the German troops by sniping at them from rooftop positions.

Tens of thousands of Jews abandoned their apartments and took refuge in the underground bunkers and sewers. The Nazi general in charge of the destruction of the Warsaw ghetto ordered German planes to drop firebombs. The ghetto was ablaze. Fierce, close-range battles raged block by block, house by house. Though vastly outnumbered, and despite the overwhelming firepower of the Nazi soldiers, the Jewish fighters continued the revolt until June, when the entire ghetto was finally razed. Some Jews escaped through the network of underground holes to the Christian side of the wall. More than 56,000 of the starving and exhausted Jews were caught and put on trains. Nearly 6,000 were killed by explosions or in fires. Hundreds, perhaps as many as 750, died in combat, from exhaustion, or by suicide. A consider-

Captured by SS troops, Jewish civilians are herded to trains bound for concentration camps.

able number of German soldiers and police officers lost their lives as well.

The Warsaw ghetto revolt was important because it encouraged other Jews to resist. It proved to partisans and guerrilla forces that small fighting units could inflict great losses upon the Nazis. For forty days, the ghetto fighters were able to prevail over enemy troops for extended periods of time. Their heroics showed they could fight with bravery and great sacrifice. Said survivor Alexander Donat, "We felt that we were resisting Nazi military force barehanded, that our refusal to surrender was no less heroic than the armed resistance of those who fought them with guns. We were co-fighters, not just fodder, excrement, meaningless sacrifices."

The resisters' determination to fight to the end inspired other Jews. It was apparent that Jews had the ability to fight with valor against seemingly insurmountable odds. After learning about the fierce resistance put up by Jewish fighters in the Warsaw ghetto, Hitler's most trusted Nazi minister, Joseph Goebbels, wrote in his diary "that it shows what one can expect of the Jews if they have guns."

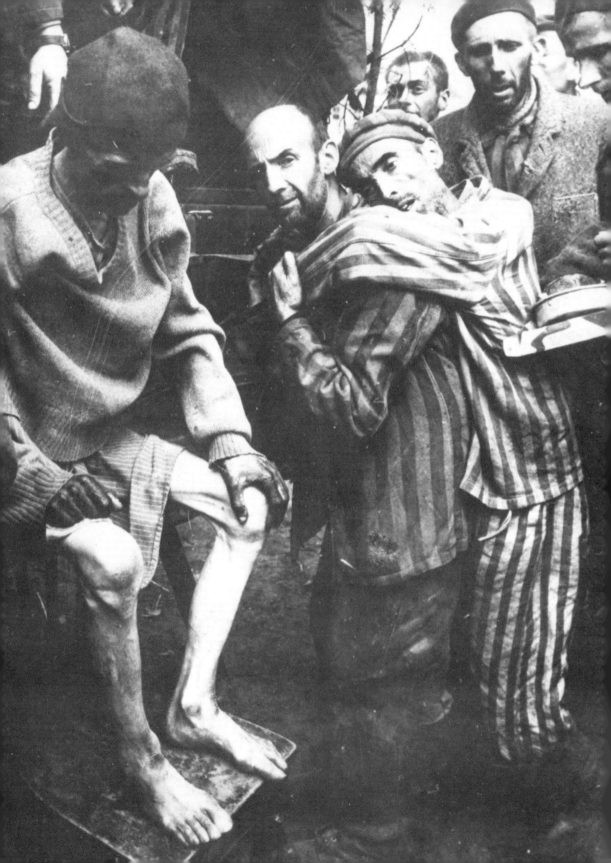

7

From Homelessness to a Homeland

BY THE MIDDLE OF JUNE 1944, Hitler's might on the battlefield had weakened further. Allied forces crossed the English Channel and invaded German-occupied France. In the south of Europe, Allied armies were defeating the Germans in their advance northward in Italy. Allied bombers were destroying cities throughout the Reich. The war had come home to German soil. German civilian and military casualties soared. Soviet counterattacks began to push Nazi troops back into Poland, and the capture of Berlin became the Soviet Union's primary objective. Worst of all for Hitler, on July 20, 1944, a group of German officers attempted to assassinate him, thinking that the killing of the Führer would end the war and stop the terrible bloodshed.

Even as total defeat loomed ahead for Hitler, his stubborn will and brutal acts of cruelty persisted. Hitler had invaded Hungary, Germany's ally, in March 1944 and had immediately ordered Eichmann to deport more than 400,000 Hungarian Jews to Auschwitz. In less than two months,

(opposite page) As Hitler's hold on Europe weakens, inmates of the Wobbelin camp are liberated.

trainloads of Jews were departing for that infamous place on a daily basis. As many as 12,000 Jews arrived every twenty-four hours. Half a million were to die there. In the face of his own catastrophes, a frenzied Hitler saw to it that the extermination of the Jews continued at an accelerated pace. With the war taking its toll, railway tracks were frequently in need of repair. Boxcars were used to evacuate Nazi soldiers from the eastern front, which prompted German officers to march their Jewish prisoners to Auschwitz and other death camps. Starting in November 1944, as many as 40,000 Jews were marched from Budapest, Hungary's capital city, to Austria. Needless to say, thousands fell by the wayside or were shot trying to escape.

Eighty thousand Jews freed

In December 1944, a little more than three months before the around-the-clock gassings of the Hungarian Jews at Auschwitz, Soviet troops penetrated the Maidanek death camp in Poland. Jewish survivors were liberated and cared for. In January 1945, as the Soviet troops took Warsaw and moved on Budapest, they were able to free eighty thousand Hungarian Jews scheduled to be sent to their death.

Realizing that they had no chance of holding back the Soviet troops, Himmler and his Nazis, fearing severe punishment at war's end, decided to take apart the Auschwitz gas chambers. The SS blew up the crematories. Then, they tried to destroy any evidence of the killings. To keep the horrors that happened there a secret, they burned camp records, clothing, and other personal property that had been collected from the Jews. At this time, the SS abandoned other concentration camps in Poland and the Baltic countries.

During the subfreezing temperatures of the

1945 winter months, the Nazis continued their relentless mass murder of Jews. Inmates from the camps being emptied in the east were forced back into Germany. Those able to march were compelled to walk as long as they could. Nearly fifty-five thousand were evacuated from Auschwitz. Those who staggered or lingered were shot. Sometimes five hundred of the marchers were shot in one day. Some froze to death; others starved. In one incident, Jews were driven into a tunnel and one thousand purposefully suffocated when the passageway was boarded up.

One of the worst of these death marches, involving some eight thousand prisoners, occurred in January 1945 on the edge of the Baltic Sea. Celia Manielewitz, a young girl at the time, later recalled:

> The Germans had started a rumor that at the coast we'd be put on board ship for Hamburg; we didn't believe it. . . . Then the rumor: The SS are driving us into the sea! This was true, we knew it at once. "We've had it," Genia [Celia's friend] whispered to me. I could only nod . . . SS men stood on the rocks to the left and right of us. They drove the prisoners to the edge of the precipice [cliff] and shot them down mercilessly. . . . We said our goodbyes. . . . "Get going!" the SS chief in charge of the operation shouted. "Get down," he yelled, "down you Jew bitches." He swung his gun and hit Genia . . . in the small of the back. She staggered and . . . an SS man pushed her over the cliff edge. . . . I saw the abyss before me and hurtled over.

Miraculously, Celia, Genia, and one other girl survived the massacre and were hidden and nursed back to health by some nearby farmers.

Liberation at last

With the war coming to a close, U.S. troops arrived at the Buchenwald and Dachau concentration camps and rescued the prisoners. British troops liberated those being held at Bergen-Belsen.

Reported historian Louis L. Snyder:

> Battle hardened veterans inured [used] to the sight and smell of death, were sickened by what they saw in these pestholes. They could scarcely believe their eyes . . . staggering out to meet them were the walking skeletons—human beings whose bodies were stripped of flesh, their eyes staring in disbelief, their voices hollow, their minds crippled by starvation and disease. Strong men wept in the presence of this miserable army of unfortunates.

On entering one of the camps, Gen. Dwight D. Eisenhower, the American commander, said that he had "never at any time experienced an equal sense of shock." Six days after the Buchenwald

In Namering, Germany, a girl breaks out in tears as she sees the exhumed bodies of eight hundred slave laborers murdered by SS guards. The bodies were laid out so that the townspeople could view the work of the Nazis.

camp was liberated, Gene Currivan of *The New York Times* witnessed a group of German civilians visiting the camp. Said Currivan:

> The German people saw all this today and they wept. . . . They said they didn't know about it. . . . Men turned white and women turned away. It was too much for them. These persons, who had been fed on Nazi propaganda since 1933, were beginning to see . . . with their own eyes what no quantity of American propaganda could convince them of. Here was what their own government had perpetrated.

In April 1945, after Soviet troops had reached the outlying parts of Berlin, the Nazis began to abandon the remaining concentration camps. Still, the Jews died. More than 400,000 of them died in the overcrowded camps, some while being forced to build the futile fortifications meant to defend the Reich to the end. And the end came on May 7, when Germany surrendered unconditionally to the Allies. Hitler's mad dream of conquest and mass murder of millions was over.

This forty-year-old man survived long enough to be liberated from Auschwitz-Birkenau in 1945.

The aftermath

A week before the war in Europe ended, Hitler and his wife, Eva Braun, killed themselves in Hitler's underground bunker below the Reich chancellery building in Berlin. They had married the day before the double suicide. Their deaths took place in Hitler's headquarters, the same complex from which he directed the Nazi war effort and ordered the killing of untold numbers of people. Toward the end of his life, Hitler had a severe stomach disorder brought on by shattered nerves. His speech was impaired, and his mind had become disoriented. He was a broken man and a shell of his former self. Himmler and Goebbels also committed suicide. None had the courage to face a court of justice.

After the war, only a small percentage of

Europe's original Jewish population survived. Had World War II lasted a few months more, or if Hitler had won the war, perhaps all of that continent's Jewish population would have been annihilated. As it turned out, the numbers of Jews murdered in each country depended on several circumstances, such as the number of Jews living in the country during the prewar years; the length of the Nazi occupation; and whether the country was a German ally. Often, the nation's leader or its people played a role in preventing the murder of the Jews. For example, Bulgarian citizens were able to protect all of Bulgaria's fifty thousand Jews from the Nazis. And in Denmark, only five hundred of its six thousand Jews were lost because the Danes secretly ferried their Jewish neighbors to Sweden.

Still, the final Jewish death toll was staggering. Of the estimated total of 5,978,000 Jews killed by the Nazis, 2,800,000 were Poles, nearly 90 percent

An inmate of the liberated Wobbelin camp is overcome when he learns that he is not leaving with the first group to the hospital.

At a concentration camp in Gotha, Germany, Gen. Dwight D. Eisenhower (middle) watches while prisoners demonstrate how they were tortured by Nazi guards.

of all the Jews who had lived in Poland before the war. Romania lost 425,000 Jews, 50 percent of its entire Jewish population. Czechoslovakia lost 260,000 (88 percent), Yugoslavia 55,000 (80 percent), Greece 60,000 (80 percent), the Netherlands 90,000 (75 percent), Belgium 40,000 (67 percent), and Hungary 200,000 (50 percent).

Shortly after the war ended, Jews tried to reestablish themselves and to renew a normal life. Some Jews, hidden by Christians, came out of hiding. Others who had retreated to the woods after escaping their ghetto or camp confinements finally left their near-primitive existence in seclusion and reappeared. A number of Jews lived out the war by fighting with partisan units. Jews who merged with the Christian communities or who relied on false baptismal papers and counterfeit identity cards were also saved. After the war, they reclaimed their Jewish names and Jewish life. Jewish orphans frequently protected by Catholic and Protestant clergy or other people were reunited with relatives. Many were turned over to

At the Bergen-Belsen camp for displaced persons, women receive armfuls of fresh bread.

Jewish organizations for eventual adoption.

Despite their liberation and Hitler's downfall, Jews continued to experience problems. Some survivors, uncertain about what to do or where to go after their liberation, decided to return to their hometowns and cities. They wanted to find their missing families, relatives, and friends. They needed to reclaim their homes and possessions. Some who returned to their homelands were shocked to learn that other people, particularly in Poland and Latvia, had taken their property and were living in their houses. When the Jews protested, some were arrested. Not only were they unwelcome but they were frequently blamed for the war and the destruction it brought to the land. In 1945 and 1946, anti-Jewish riots broke out in Polish cities. Several hundred Jews were murdered.

S.L. Schneiderman witnessed the massacre of dozens of Jews in Kielce, Poland, during a peaceful meeting at a Jewish home:

> Stones came crashing through the windows. An infuriated mob broke into the house, beat the Jews with iron bars and axes, and hurled the victims through the windows to the crowd outside, which trampled them to death.

These anti-Jewish outbursts convinced 100,000 Jews to flee Poland and the surrounding countries once and for all.

Slave laborers

The Jews also fled Europe to avoid becoming slave laborers. The Soviets, in their quest to establish communism throughout the continent, if not the world, began to occupy most of the nations between East Germany and the Soviet Union. Some countries were forced to establish communist governments that took their orders from Kremlin officials in Moscow.

In order to rebuild their war-ravaged cities, the Soviets placed tens of thousands of slave laborers and war prisoners in work battalions and moved them around the Soviet Union and eastern Europe. They were held as captives in the postwar years. For fear of being used as slave laborers, thousands of homeless and stateless Jews and others fled into West Germany, where the Allies had set up separate occupation zones that were administered by military governments. These liberated but not yet free people were called displaced persons. By the end of the war, there were ten million Jewish and non-Jewish displaced persons wandering around Europe. Their lives were shattered. Food, clothing, and medical supplies were hard to come by, and many therefore died. Some had to stay in the concentration camps. By 1946, over 200,000 Jewish survivors were placed in displaced persons camps, but now these camps were administered by the United Nations Relief Organization and Allied armies. The camps, unlike the Nazi camps, were designed to save, rather than kill, displaced persons.

Unfortunately, there was much bickering

Surviving children show their tattoos—identification numbers permanently etched onto their forearms.

Seeking refuge, a Jewish family emigrates to France at the end of the war.

among the various army, government, and private agencies on how to take care of the displaced and what was to be done with them. This confusion made it difficult for the Jews to begin rebuilding their lives. The Jews who had survived the Holocaust needed to settle into homes so that they could reestablish normal lives and deal with their emotional scars, including guilt. Survivors frequently wondered why they had been spared when two out of every three European Jews had been murdered.

Israel becomes home to the displaced persons

Many Jews had tried to escape from Europe during the war. As many as 238,000 Jews managed to flee Germany. Another 118,000 left Austria. Additionally, tens of thousands decided to uproot themselves from other European countries and seek out a safer nation in which to start a new life.

After the war ended, Jewish displaced persons again sought refuge in other countries from their war-torn lives. Many countries, however, had strict immigration quotas. Others simply did not want the Jews.

In an attempt to help find the Jews a home, the newly formed United Nations recommended that they be resettled in Palestine in the Middle East. Palestine seemed a natural choice because Jews had historic ties to the land and because Zionist Jews had been immigrating to Palestine since the 1880s. Because of the large number of Arabs living in the area, it was suggested that Palestine be partitioned into Jewish and Arab states. The issue came before the United Nations General Assembly in 1947 and, after much debate, the state of Israel was created on May 14, 1948. The Arabs, however, protested the establishment of a Jewish state in Palestine and war resulted when the armies of five neighboring Arab states invaded Israel. After a final armistice, or truce, was signed in 1949, Jews were encouraged to settle in Israel. By 1951, more than half of the European Jewish displaced persons had immigrated to the new country.

Jewish immigrants leave for Israel on the Exodus *in 1947.*

In Israel and throughout the world, Jews vow that the Holocaust should never be repeated. And they will never let the memory of the horror fade into the past. Late in March or early April, a special day is set aside the world over to ponder the fate of the Jews throughout Europe during the time of Hitler. This day is called Yom Hashoa. The Israeli parliament also built a permanent monument on Mount Remembrance in Jerusalem. It is named Yad Vashem, Martyrs' and Heroes' Remembrance Museum. An eternal flame burns there to remind the millions of visitors to the museum of the perseverance and continuation of the Jewish people. The museum's statues and exhibits help tell the dreadful, true story of the Holocaust.

8

People to Remember and Lessons to Recall

THE MAJORITY of the world's population was unaware of what was happening to the Jews in Europe during the Hitler era. Many others stood by without protesting as their Jewish neighbors were being persecuted, sent away, and murdered. Some even cooperated with the Nazis in their war against the Jews. On the other hand, thousands of courageous and compassionate non-Jews risked their lives to save Jews during the Holocaust. These individuals are known as "righteous gentiles." On the grounds of Yad Vashem, hundreds of trees line the Avenue of Righteous Gentiles. Each tree was planted to honor those who were brave enough to hide Jews or to smuggle them to safe locations. In a number of instances, their heroic deeds prevented Jews from being deported.

(opposite page) With the reign of Nazi terror over, two survivors cut the yellow stars from their clothing.

Saving Jews

The countries of Bulgaria and Denmark displayed distinguished records in saving their Jews. In Bulgaria, public outcry prevented Bulgarian

Danish Jews set sail for Sweden. With the help of their countrymen, many Denmark Jews escaped death at Nazi hands.

Jews from being sent to Auschwitz. Citizens sent thousands of letters to the Bulgarian parliament protesting harsh treatment of Jews. Three bishops of the Bulgarian Orthodox Church preached against anti-Semitism. They sent warnings to the Nazi occupiers not to deport Bulgarian Jews. There was a large, violent street demonstration in favor of the Jews. Some historians contend that King Boris deliberately delayed the Nazis from sending the Jews out of his country. At war's end, forty-five thousand of Bulgaria's fifty thousand Jews left for Israel, where they proudly acknowledge the Bulgarian people's role in protecting the Jewish population.

Denmark

In Denmark in October 1943, there was a most daring and dramatic rescue of more than six thousand Danish Jews. Just days before the notorious Gestapo planned a surprise roundup of all of Denmark's Jews, word of the secret plan was uncovered by some Danes. The Danish community then warned the Jews that they were about to be sent to the camps in the east. With the exception of six hundred older Jews who were unable to escape, the rest of the Danish Jews were placed in prearranged hiding places along the coast. In a cleverly designed operation, the Jews were concealed in the holds of a flotilla of fishing boats. At great risk of being sighted by Nazi patrol boats, the Danes ferried the Jews across a twenty-four mile strait to neutral Sweden, where they were able to live until the war was over.

Throughout every country in Europe, even in Germany, there were those who helped Jews escape and hide. Those who were found out were killed. In Poland, where the largest number of Jews died, Poles hid Jews and shared their own scarce amounts of food. Organized groups such as the Christian clergy, Socialists, Communists, and anti-Nazi nationalist partisans often undertook campaigns to save Jews. Sympathetic friends provided safe houses in rural areas.

Although the Vatican did not officially condemn the Nazi atrocities, there is considerable evidence that many priests, nuns, and lay Catholics hid Jews in monasteries, convents, schools, and hospitals. Especially in southern France and Italy, many thousands of children were safely guarded or smuggled into Spain or Switzerland, two nations not involved in the war. In the small, wine-producing French town of Le Chambon, Jews were rescued and hidden. When the villagers refused to reveal to the Nazis where the Jews were being held, every one of the townspeople was arrested and tortured.

In Greece, Jews were taken to mountain hide-outs or hidden on islands. Some were smuggled into Turkey. In Italy, the Italian army rescued and protected Jews. Police in Italy were very helpful in making sure Italian Jews were shielded from the Nazis. One chief of police was actually deported to Dachau and executed for having helped Jews. It was not uncommon to find Italian government officials and Italian people acting to prevent Jews

Women and children from the liberated camp at Lambach, Austria.

Although she did not survive the Holocaust, Anne Frank left her diary as a legacy. In it, she poignantly describes her years in hiding from the Nazis in Amsterdam, Holland.

from being handed over to the Germans. In Yugoslavia, a band of Serbs raided a concentration camp and freed some of the Jews. In Belgium, railway workers attacked a train leaving for Auschwitz, which enabled hundreds of Jews on board to escape their fate. In another incident, the king of Morocco refused to turn over 300,000 Jews of that country to the pro-Nazi government that ran France after it surrendered to Germany. In Finland, the government boldly refused to adopt an anti-Jewish policy. Norway's people and national church defied the Nazis and blocked efforts to have Jews arrested and deported.

Anne Frank

In the Netherlands, as in other countries occupied by the Germans, Jews were made to wear a yellow Star of David as an identity badge. But the Dutch reaction to seeing people wearing the star was to cheer the Jews and encourage them in their struggle. In the Netherlands, there was a very active underground that worked to protect its Jews. Yet there were paid informers here, too. One informer in Amsterdam betrayed a teenage Dutch girl, Anne Frank, and her family for a few guilders. The Franks had been safely hidden in a concealed attic by a Christian friend for two years. When they were discovered, they were sent away. Anne died at Bergen-Belsen. The entire family, except for the father, perished at the hands of the Nazis. Anne Frank's extremely sensitive diary describes hiding from the Nazis, and she writes about her dreams for a life that was never realized. "Surely," she wrote, "the time will come when we are people again, and not just Jews." Her optimism about humanity was apparent when she wrote, "In spite of everything I believe that people are really good at heart." Anne Frank's story has been read by millions of school children all over the world. The site of her hiding place in Amsterdam has been visited by many millions as well, and there they pause to reflect on the Holocaust tragedy.

Raoul Wallenberg, serving as a Swedish diplomat in Hungary in 1944, saved thousands of Jews. By buying buildings in Budapest and flying Swedish flags over them, he placed them under the authority of the Swedish government. Wallenberg then invited Jews to enter the houses and live under the protective custody of Sweden. He also created forged papers that gave the Jews passports to leave Hungary as Swedish citizens. The Gestapo tried to kill Wallenberg and when the Soviet army entered Hungary, he mysteriously disappeared.

Hundreds of bodies line the yard of the Gestapo concentration camp at Lager Nordhausen.

(left to right) Göring, Hess, von Ribbentrop, and Keitel sit in the front row at the Nuremberg trials, where they are accused of committing war crimes.

After the war, many of the leaders of the Third Reich were captured by the Allies and were placed on trial in Nuremberg, Germany, for committing war crimes. The court sessions lasted for eleven months, from November 1945 to October 1946. The judges in this world-famous trial disregarded the defendants' pleas that they should not be blamed for following Hitler's orders. Nineteen of the Nazis were found guilty of enslavement and murder and of violating "international moral laws" against peace. Twelve of these were hanged. Air Marshal Hermann Göring committed suicide. Later, smaller trials were held over the years, and more than eighty thousand Germans were convicted of committing crimes against humanity. Many local criminals and Nazi collaborators in various countries occupied by the Germans were brought to justice and sentenced for their crimes. Even in Germany, six thousand Germans were convicted for the crimes committed, but lighter punishments were handed out there.

Some fled punishment

The case of Adolf Eichmann and his crimes was loaded with intrigue. Eichmann was the field coordinator of the Nazi concentration and extermination camps. He was arrested at the end of World War II by U.S. soldiers, but he escaped and went underground, living a life of disguise and hiding in Argentina. In May 1960, members of the Israeli Secret Service tracked him down in Argentina and smuggled him to Israel. He was put on trial in Jerusalem a year later, convicted of his cowardly and dreadful crimes, and executed on May 31, 1962.

At the conclusion of the war, Josef Mengele also dropped out of sight and fled to South America, where other Nazis took refuge. He was able to successfully hide from his pursuers for nearly thirty-five years. In 1985, it was revealed that he drowned in 1979 while swimming in Brazil.

Practically all Germans now regret that the Nazis once came to power in their country. It is a dark chapter in their history. For many years, Germany has accepted blame for Nazi crimes and has admitted its responsibility for the Holocaust. The government has paid billions of German marks in reparations to Israel and to Jewish individuals. Reparations are payments made for wrongdoing and for losses suffered by those who have been injured.

The people who lived through the horrors of the Holocaust believe that each new generation should be thoroughly educated about what the Nazis did. They hope that this knowledge will keep such atrocities from being committed in the future. The events of the Holocaust reveal graphically that

German Air Marshal Hermann Göring committed suicide following his conviction at Nuremberg.

some people have the capacity for committing inhumane acts against others. Said Viktor Frankl, who survived one of the Nazi death camps, "Life in a concentration camp tore open the human soul and exposed its depths. . . . The rift dividing good from evil, which goes through all human beings . . . is laid open by the concentration camp." In such an extreme situation, Frankl seems to be saying, it is revealed who is moral and who is without morals, who is compassionate for fellow human beings and who is cold-hearted and brutal.

Another lesson of the Nazi crimes is that it is morally wrong to remain silent in the face of evil. Many people knew what was happening in the death camps but did not speak out or try to get word to people in other countries. This allowed the Nazis to continue with their killing. Many

After the war, many Holocaust victims were exhumed from the mass graves where they had been dumped so they could be given a dignified burial.

who committed these mass murders claimed they were only following orders given by their superiors. This excuse was not accepted at the trials of Nazi criminals after the war. The Allied judges stated that there are some orders which are so terrible and immoral that they must be disobeyed, even in the face of death.

The German writer Gerhard Schoenberner has spoken often about the guilt that Germans must bear for what their countrymen did during World War II. He believes, just as do many Jews and other concerned people, that the Holocaust must never be forgotten. "There remains a shared guilt," he says, "which one cannot easily buy oneself out of, and which cannot be 'made good.' No one can bring the dead back to life. What is done cannot be undone."

Civilians give burial to eight hundred victims of an SS killing.

But humanity can and must remember, says Schoenberner. What happened must be constantly laid bare and examined, the horrors repeatedly retold so that young people with no memory of those times will know the awful truth. "Belated moral condemnation and human regret are not enough," Schoenberner insists. He says:

> The historical facts must be made known, the social causes that made them possible must be understood, and we must become aware of our own responsibility for what goes on around us. We do not escape the past by thrusting it to the back of our minds. Only if we come to terms with it and understand the lessons of those years, can we free ourselves of the legacy of Hitlerite barbarism.

Chronology of Events

1933

January 30	Adolf Hitler appointed chancellor of Germany.
March 22	Dachau concentration camp opens.
April 1	Boycott of Jewish shops and businesses.
April 7	Laws for reestablishment of the civil service bar Jews from holding civil service, university, and state positions.
April 26	Gestapo established.
May 10	Public burnings of books written by Jews, political dissidents, and others not approved by the state.
July 14	Law strips east European Jewish immigrants of German citizenship.

1934

August 2	Hitler proclaims himself Führer and Reich chancellor. Armed forces must now swear allegiance to him.

1935

May 31	Jews barred from serving in the German armed forces.
September 15- November 15	Anti-Jewish racial laws, called Nuremberg laws, enacted. Jews no longer considered German citizens. Jews not allowed to marry Aryans or fly the German flag. Germany issues a detailed definition of who constitutes a Jew.

1936

March 3	Jewish doctors barred from practicing medicine in German institutions.
March 7	Germans march into the Rhineland, previously demilitarized by the Treaty of Versailles.
June 17	Heinrich Himmler appointed the chief of German police.
October 25	Hitler and Benito Mussolini form Rome-Berlin Axis.

1937

July 15	Buchenwald concentration camp opens.

1938

March 13	Austria is annexed by the German Reich (the *Anschluss*). All anti-Semitic decrees immediately applied in Austria.
April 26	Mandatory registration of all property held by Jews inside the Reich.
August 1	Adolf Eichmann establishes the Office of Jewish Emigration in Vienna to increase the pace of forced emigration.
September 30	Munich Conference: England and France agree to German occupation of the Sudetenland, previously western Czechoslovakia.
October 5	Following request by Swiss authorities, Germans mark all Jewish passports with a large letter *J* to restrict Jews from immigrating to Switzerland.
October 28	Seventeen thousand Polish Jews living in Germany are expelled. Poles refuse to admit them and eight thousand are stranded in the frontier village of Zbaszyn.
November 9-10	*Kristallnacht*, or the night of broken glass. Anti-Jewish pogrom in Germany, Austria, and the Sudetenland. Two hundred synagogues destroyed, seventy-five hundred Jewish shops looted, and thirty thousand male Jews sent to concentration camps (Dachau, Buchenwald, Sachsenhausen).
November 12	Decree forcing all Jews to transfer retail businesses to Aryans.
November 15	All Jewish pupils expelled from German schools.
December 12	Fine of one billion marks levied against German Jews for the destruction of property during *Kristallnacht*.

1939

January 30	Hitler claims in Reichstag speech that if war erupts, it will mean the extermination of European Jews.
March 15	Germans occupy Czechoslovakia.
August 23	Nonaggression pact (Molotov-Ribbentrop Pact) signed between the Soviet Union and Germany.
September 1	Beginning of World War II: Germany invades Poland.
September 21	Reinhard Heydrich issues directives to establish ghettos in German-occupied Poland.
October 28	First Polish ghetto established in Piotrkow.
November 23	Jews in German-occupied Poland forced to wear an arm band or star.

1940

April 9	Germans occupy Denmark and southern Norway.
May 7	Lodz ghetto sealed: 165,000 people contained in 1.6 square miles.

May 10	Germany invades the Netherlands, Belgium, Luxembourg, and France.
May 20	Concentration camps established at Auschwitz.
June 22	France surrenders.
August 8	Battle of Britain begins.
September 27	Rome-Berlin-Tokyo Axis formed.
November 15	Warsaw ghetto sealed: ultimately contained 500,00 people.

1941

January 21-26	Anti-Jewish riots in Romania where hundreds of Jews are butchered.
March	Adolf Eichmann appointed head of Gestapo department for Jewish affairs.
April 6	Germany attacks Yugoslavia and Greece; occupation follows.
June 22	Germany invades the Soviet Union.
July 31	Heydrich appointed by Hermann Göring to implement the "final solution."
September 28-29	Over thirty-four thousand Jews massacred at Babi Yar outside Kiev.
October	Establishment of Auschwitz II for the extermination of Jews. Gypsies, Poles, Soviets, and others were also murdered at the camp.
December 7	Japanese attack Pearl Harbor.
December 8	Chelmno extermination camp begins operations: 340,000 Jews and 20,000 Poles and Czechs murdered by April 1943.

1942

January 20	Wannsee Conference in Berlin: Heydrich outlines plan to murder Europe's Jews.
March 17	Extermination begins in Belzec; by end of 1942, 600,000 Jews murdered.
May	Extermination by gas begins in Sobibor killing center; by October 1943, 250,000 Jews murdered.
June	Jewish partisan units established in the forests of Belorussia and the Baltic states.
Summer	Deportation of Jews to killing centers from Belgium, Croatia, France, the Netherlands, and Poland. Armed resistance by Jews in the Russian ghettos of Kletzk, Kremenetes, Lachwa, Mir, Tuchin, and Weizweiz.
Winter	Deportation of Jews from Germany, Greece, and Norway to killing centers. Jewish partisan movement organized in forests near Lublin, Poland.

1943

January	German Sixth Army surrenders at Stalingrad.
March	Destruction of Krakow ghetto.
April	Warsaw ghetto revolt begins as Germans attempt to remove seventy thousand inhabitants. Jewish underground fights Nazis until early June.
June	Himmler orders the liquidation of all ghettos in Poland and the Soviet Union.
Summer	Armed resistance by Jews in Czestochowa, Lvov, Bedzin, Bialystok, and Tarnow ghettos in Poland.
Fall	Liquidation of large ghettos in Minsk, Vilna, and Riga in the Soviet Union.
October 14	Armed revolt in Sobibor extermination camp.

1944

March 19	Germany occupies Hungary.
May 15	Nazis begin deporting Hungarian Jews; by June 27, 380,000 sent to Auschwitz.
June 6	Allied invasion at Normandy, France.
Spring/Summer	Soviet army repels Nazi forces.
July 20	Group of German officers attempts to assassinate Hitler.
July 24	Soviets liberate Maidanek killing center in Poland.
October 7	Revolt by inmates at Auschwitz; one crematory blown up.
November	Last Jews deported from Theresienstadt to Auschwitz.
November 8	Beginning of death march of approximately forty thousand Jews from Budapest to Austria.

1945

January 17	Evacuation of Auschwitz; beginning of death march.
January 25	Beginning of death march for inmates of Stutthof, Poland.
April 6-10	Death march for inmates of Buchenwald.
April 30	Hitler commits suicide.
May 8	Germany surrenders; end of Third Reich.

Glossary

Allied nations: The countries fighting Nazi Germany and fascist Italy during World War II; primarily the United States, Great Britain, the Soviet Union, and to a lesser degree, France.

anti-Semitism: Dislike of, or prejudice against Jews, often accompanied by active discrimination or persecution of Jewish people.

Aryan: A person of northern European racial background; term used by the Nazis to indicate the white German race, which they deemed to be superior.

blitzkrieg: A sudden, swift, large-scale military attack intended to win a quick victory; used by the Nazis in World War II.

brownshirts: Storm troopers, or members of Hitler's Nazi Party militia, notorious for their brutal and terrorist methods.

Communists: Members of the Communist party and dedicated to the establishment of an economic system in which ownership of all property is by and for the community.

concentration camps: Detention camps established to hold all enemies of the Nazis. Though millions of people died in these camps, they were not originally designed to be killing centers.

crematory: A building with a furnace for burning dead bodies; used by the Nazis for cremating the remains of death camp prisoners.

deportation: The removal of Jews in German-occupied countries. Jews were told they were to be "resettled" elsewhere, but most were sent to concentration or death camps.

displaced persons: Those people forced from their countries as a result of war and left homeless. Many survivors of the Holocaust were often placed in special camps for displaced persons.

***Einsatzgruppen*:** Mobile killing squads of the security police and SS security service attached to the German army. At least one million Jews in eastern Europe and the Soviet Union were shot by these units and buried in mass graves.

"final solution": Name of the Nazi program to destroy the Jews of Europe.

Führer: The German word for "leader." It was a title assumed by Adolf Hitler when he became head of the Nazi party. The term implies tremendous prestige and power.

gas chamber: Rooms in sealed-off buildings in death camps in which large numbers of people were killed with poison gas.

genocide: A systematic killing intended to destroy a whole national or ethnic group, such as the Nazi attempt to exterminate the Jews.

Gestapo: The secret police force of the German Nazi state; a branch of the SS that dealt harshly with all opponents by using terrorism and committing atrocities.

ghetto: The section of certain European cities in which Jews were required to live under restricted conditions.

Gypsies: Members of a wandering people, originally from northwest India, usually with dark skin and black hair, found throughout the world.

guerrilla warfare: A type of warfare in which a small band of defensive soldiers, usually volunteers, makes surprise raids or sabotages an invading army.

Holocaust: A great or total destruction of life. The term is often used to refer to the destruction of some six million Jews by the Nazis and their followers in Europe between 1933 and 1945.

***Judenrat*:** Council of Jewish representatives established in communities and ghettos by the Nazis to carry out Nazi orders and to administer Jewish life.

Kristallnacht: Also called the "night of broken glass"; A mass riot unleashed by the Nazis against Jews and Jewish institutions in Germany and Austria on November 9 and 10, 1938. As a result, thirty-five thousand men were sent to concentration camps.

Nazi: Abbreviation for the National Socialist German Workers' Party, the German fascist political organization founded in 1919 and promoted by Hitler. It advocated nationalism, racism, rearmament, and aggression in Germany.

partisans: Guerrilla fighters engaged in attacking an invading enemy. During World War II the term was applied to all resistance fighters in Nazi-occupied countries.

propaganda: The systematic, widespread distribution of particular ideas, doctrines, or practices to promote a cause or to damage an opposing one.

Reich: The German government. The German fascist state under the Nazis from 1933 to 1945 was the Third Reich.

Reichstag: The name of the former legislative assembly of Germany.

righteous gentiles: Term applied to those non-Jews who saved or tried to save Jews from their Nazi persecutors at the risk of their own lives.

SS: Abbreviation for *Schutzstaffel*, the protective units initially organized as Hitler's personal bodyguards. Under Heinrich Himmler, they later served as battle troops and were best known for trying to carry out the destruction of the European Jewry.

storm troopers: Members of Hitler's Nazi party militia who were notorious for their brutal and terrorist methods.

Treaty of Versailles: A treaty signed at the end of World War I that took away considerable German territory and forced that country to pay reparations to the Allies. It also blamed Germany for starting the war.

Yiddish: A language derived from medieval High German spoken by east European Jews. It is written in the Hebrew alphabet and contains vocabulary from Hebrew, Russian,

Polish, English, and other languages.

Zionist: A member of a movement in favor of the reestablishment and support of the Jewish national state of Israel.

Organizations to Contact

The following organizations sponsor activities and programs about the Holocaust. Most often, their facilities include resource centers, collections, exhibits, publications, educational outreach programs, and the sponsorship of commemorative observances, conferences, and speakers' bureaus.

Board of Jewish Education of Greater New York—The Pedagogic Resource Center
426 W. 58th St.
New York, NY 10019
(212) 245-8200

The Board of Jewish Education offers commemorative and educational programs on the Holocaust. Every two years, it features the March of the Living, where high school students from all over the United States travel to Poland, Germany, and Israel, learning about the history of the Jewish nation. The Board has published *Kristallnacht Resource Guide*, a book about the Holocaust.

Braun Center for Holocaust Studies (BCHS)
c/o Anti-Defamation League of B'nai B'rith
823 United Nations Plaza
New York, NY 10017
(212) 490-2525

BCHS provides information on the Holocaust. Its archives include over three thousand books, as well as films, videos, and newspaper clippings. The Center also develops curriculum dealing with the Holocaust, and organizes teacher-training workshops. It publishes *Dimensions: A Journal of Holocaust Studies* three times a year; and *The Holocaust: Catalog of Publications and Audio-Visual Materials*.

Facing History and Ourselves National Foundation (FHONF)
25 Kennard Rd.
Brookline, MA 02146
(617) 232-1595

FHONF develops curriculum at the junior-high, high-school, and university levels. The curriculum is designed to encourage critical thinking about the lessons of the Holocaust. The Foundation maintains a library that includes books, films, survivor testimony, and research projects. The Foundation publishes the periodical *Facing History and Ourselves.*

Holocaust Memorial Foundation of Illinois (HMFI)
4255 Main St.
Skokie, IL 60076
(708) 677-4640

HMFI is an educational and resource center, and offers teacher-training courses on the Holocaust. The resource center also features a library containing books on the Holocaust from 1933 to 1945, transcripts of the Nuremberg Trials, and a pictorial exhibit of the Warsaw ghetto. The Foundation publishes *Foundation Monthly* and a five-day curriculum on the Holocaust at the high-school level.

Holocaust Survivors Memorial Foundation (HSMF)
350 Fifth Ave., Suite 3508
New York, NY 10118
(212) 594-8765

HSMF consists of Holocaust survivors, children of survivors, and American Jews. The Foundation seeks to teach Americans about the history and current implications of the Holocaust. It holds community conferences, sponsors research, and translates Holocaust literature, including poetry, songs, and diaries composed in the ghettos and concentration camps. The Foundation holds a monthly discussion group and an annual convention.

Museum of Jewish Heritage—A Living Memorial to the Holocaust (MJH)
342 Madison Ave., Suite 706
New York, NY 10713
(212) 687-9141

MJH will open its museum to the public in 1992, and will feature four permanent exhibits: The World Before, The Holocaust, The

Aftermath, and Renewal in America. The Museum will also feature a memorial hall dedicated to the six million Jews who lost their lives in the Holocaust, and a computerized learning center. Available now from the Museum are its bimonthly publication *Museum Newsletter* and assorted brochures.

National Conference of Christians and Jews (NCCJ)
71 Fifth Ave., Suite 1100
New York, NY 10003-3095
(212) 206-0006

NCCJ seeks to bring together individuals from all religious groups to promote interfaith relations and equal opportunity in industry. It publishes the annual newsletter *National Conference of Christians and Jews*.

Simon Wiesenthal Center (SWC)
9760 W. Pico Blvd.
Los Angeles, CA 90035
(310) 553-9036

SWC seeks to educate students on the history and lessons of the Holocaust and to combat the ignorance and prejudice that caused it. SWC maintains a twenty thousand volume library and archival collection and publishes the quarterly newsletter *Response* and the *Simon Wiesenthal Center Annual*.

United States Holocaust Memorial Council (USHMC)
2000 L St. NW, Suite 588
Washington, DC 20036
(202) 653-9220

USHMC was established to implement the recommendations of the President's Commission on the Holocaust. The Council works for the construction of a national Holocaust historical museum, and the implementation of an annual civic commemoration of the Holocaust. It publishes the periodical *Directory of Holocaust Resource Centers, Institutions, and Organizations in North America*.

Suggestions for Further Reading

David A. Altshuler, *Hitler's War Against the Jews*. New York: Behrman House Inc., 1978.

John Bierman, *Righteous Gentile: The Story of Raoul Wallenberg, Missing Hero of the Holocaust*. New York: Viking Penguin, 1981.

Charity Blackstock, *The Children*. Boston: Little, Brown & Co. Inc., 1966.

Ayriel Eisenberg, ed., *The Lost Generation: Children in the Holocaust*. New York: Pilgrim Press, 1982.

Gerald Fleming, *Hitler and the Final Solution*. Berkeley: University of California Press, 1984.

Harold Flender, *Rescue in Denmark*. New York: Simon & Schuster, 1963.

Anne Frank, *The Diary of a Young Girl*. New York: Doubleday, 1967.

Yisrael Gutman, *The Jews of Warsaw, 1939-1943: Ghetto, Underground, Revolt*. Bloomington: Indiana University Press, 1982.

Kitty Hart, *Return to Auschwitz*. New York: Atheneum Publishers, 1982.

Judy Hoffman, *Joseph and Me: In the Days of the Holocaust*. New York: KTAV Publishing House Inc., 1979.

William Loren Katz, *An Album of Nazism*. New York: Franklin Watts Inc., 1979.

Milton Meltzer, *Never to Forget: The Jews of the Holocaust*. New York: Harper & Row Publishers Inc., 1976.

Milton Meltzer, *Rescue: The Story of How Gentiles Saved Jews in the Holocaust*. New York: Harper & Row Publishers Inc., 1988.

William Mishell, *Kadish for Kovno: Life and Death in a Lithuanian Ghetto*. Chicago: Chicago Review Press Inc., 1988.

Anne E. Neimark, *One Man's Valor: Leo Baeck and the Holocaust*. New York: E.P. Dutton, 1986.

Iris Noble, *Nazi Hunter, Simon Wiesenthal*. New York: Julian Messner, 1979.

Catherine Hanf Noren, *The Camera of My Family*. New York: Alfred A. Knopf Inc., 1976.

Jona Oberski, *Childhood: A Remembrance*. New York: Doubleday, 1983.

Doris Orgel, *The Devil in Vienna*. New York: Dial Books for Young Readers, 1978.

Judah Pilch, ed., *The Jewish Catastrophe in Europe*. New York: American Association for Jewish Education, 1968.

Sabine Reichel, *What Did You Do in the War, Daddy?* New York: Hill and Wang, 1989.

Seymour Rossel, *The Holocaust*. New York: Franklin Watts Inc., 1981.

Arnold P. Rubin, *The Evil That Men Do: The Story of the Nazis*. New York: Bantam Books, 1979.

Maxine Schur, *Hannah Szenes: A Song of Light*. Philadelphia: Jewish Publication Society, 1986.

Aranka Siegal, *Upon the Head of the Goat: A Childhood in Hungary, 1939-1944*. New York: Farrar, Straus & Giroux Inc., 1981.

John Toland, *Adolf Hitler*. New York: Doubleday, 1976.

Elie Wiesel, *Legends of Our Time*. New York: Henry Holt & Co. Inc., 1968.

Rose Zar, *In the Mouth of the Wolf*. Philadelphia: Jewish Publication Society, 1983.

Works Consulted

Yehuda Bauer, *Flight and Rescue*. New York: Random House Inc., 1970.

Lucy S. Dawidowicz, *From That Place and Time*. New York: W.W. Norton & Co. Inc., 1989.

Lucy S. Dawidowicz, *The War Against the Jews, 1933-1945*. New York: Henry Holt & Co. Inc., 1975.

Terrence Des Pres, *The Survivor: An Anatomy of Life in the Death Camps*. New York: Oxford University Press Inc., 1976.

Azriel Eisenberg, *Witness to the Holocaust*. New York: The Pilgrim Press, 1981.

Konnilyn G. Feig, *Hitler's Death Camps: The Sanity of Madness*. New York: Holmes & Meier Publishers Inc., 1981.

Albert H. Friedlander, *Out of the Whirlwind*. New York: Union of American Hebrew Congregations, 1968.

Martin Gilbert, *Final Journey: The Fate of the Jews in Nazi Europe*. New York: Mayflower Books, 1979.

Martin Gilbert, *The Holocaust: A History of the Jews of Europe During the Second World War*. New York: Henry Holt & Co. Inc., 1986.

Martin Gilbert, *The Macmillan Atlas of the Holocaust*. New York: Macmillan Publishing Co., 1982.

Alex Grobman and Daniel Landes, eds., *Critical Issues of the Holocaust*. Los Angeles: The Simon Wiesenthal Center, 1983.

Raul Hilberg, *The Destruction of the European Jews*. Chicago: Quadrangle Press, 1961.

Nora Levin, *The Holocaust: The Destruction of European*

Jewry, 1933-1945. New York: Thomas Y. Crowell Company, 1968.

Jacob Reitinger, *The Final Solution: The Attempt to Exterminate the Jews of Europe, 1939-1945.* New York: A.S. Barnes, 1961.

William Shirer, *The Rise and Fall of the Third Reich.* New York: Random House, Inc., 1961.

Arad Yitzhak, *Belzec, Sobibor, Treblinka: The Operation Reinhard Death Camps.* Bloomington: Indiana University Press, 1987.

Index

Picture Credits

Cover photo by Simon Wiesenthal Center Archives, Los Angeles, CA
Adolf Hitler: Bilder aus dem Leben des Führers, Hamburg: Herausgegeben
  Vom Cigaretten, 1936/Simon Wiesenthal Center Archives, Los Angeles, CA, 12,
  19
Archives of the State Museum, Oswiecim/Simon Wiesenthal Center Archives,
  Los Angeles, CA, 57, 58
Archive Agencije za Fotodokumentaci ju Zagrebu/Simon Wiesenthal Center
  Archives, Los Angeles, CA, 51
Auschwitz Memorial Museum/Bildarchiv Preussischer Kulturbesitz/Simon
  Wiesenthal Center Archives, Los Angeles, CA, 54, 95
Auschwitz Memorial Museum/Simon Wiesenthal Center Archives, Los Angeles,
  CA, 91, 95
Bet Lohame Ha - Geta'ot/Simon Wiesenthal Center Archives, Los Angeles, CA,
  26, 29, 75
Bildarchiv Preussischer Kulterbesitz/Simon Wiesenthal Center Archives, Los
  Angeles, CA, 24, 30, 36 (bottom), 47, 60, 97
Bundesarchiv/Simon Wiesenthal Center Archives, Los Angeles, CA, 39, 41, 45
Bundesarchiv Koblenz/Simon Wiesenthal Center Archives, Los Angeles, CA,
  23, 34, 42
Dachau Concentration Camp Memorial/Simon Wiesenthal Center Archives, Los
  Angeles, CA, 8, 78
Der Stuermer, January 1934/Simon Wiesenthal Center Archives, Los Angeles,
  CA, 21
Deutschland Erwacht/Simon Wiesenthal Center Archives, Los Angeles, CA, 17,
  22, 105
Documentation Archives of the Austrian Resistance, Vienna/Simon Wiesenthal
  Center Archives, Los Angeles, CA, 11
Ein Bilderbuch fuer Gross und Klein, Nuremberg, 1936/Simon Wiesenthal
  Center Archives, Los Angeles, CA, 20
Hebrew Immigrant Aid Society/Simon Wiesenthal Center Archives, Los Angeles,
  CA, 96
Kulturgeschichtliches Museum, Osnabrück/Simon Wiesenthal Center Archives,
  Los Angeles, CA, 74
Leo Baeck Institute/Simon Wiesenthal Center Archives, Los Angeles, CA, 38
Mauthausen Memorial/Simon Wiesenthal Center Archives, Los Angeles, CA, 79
Museum of Denmark's Flight for Freedom, 1940-1945, Copenhagen/Simon
  Wiesenthal Center Archives, Los Angeles, CA, 100
NARA/Simon Wiesenthal Center Archives, Los Angeles, CA, 63, 83
National Archives, 14, 15, 16, 33, 36 (top), 48, 50, 56, 59, 62, 64, 65, 66, 67, 70,
  72, 76, 77, 82, 84, 86, 90, 92, 93, 101, 103, 104, 106, 107
National Archives/Simon Wiesenthal Center Archives, Los Angeles, CA, 80, 98
Simon Wiesenthal Center Archives, Los Angeles, CA, 28, 32, 102
Stadarchiva Bielefeld/Simon Wiesenthal Center Archives, Los Angeles, CA, 52
Stichting Nederlands Foto & Grafisch Centrum/Simon Wiesenthal Center
  Archives, Los Angeles, CA, 32
World Federation, Bergen-Belsen Survivors/Simon Wiesenthal Center Archives,
  Los Angeles, CA, 94
Yad Vashem/Simon Wiesenthal Center Archives, Los Angeles, CA, 37

About the Author

Abraham Resnick, a native of New Jersey, is an award-winning author and educator specializing in elementary and secondary social studies education. His many writings include textbooks and trade books for students. Dr. Resnick is a professor of education at Jersey City State College in New Jersey and for many years was Director of the Instructional Materials Center at Rutgers University Graduate School of Education. In 1975, he received that school's Alumni Award for Distinguished Service to Education.